£3.99

Ashok Banker

BOLLYWOOD

www.pocketessentials.com

First published in Great Britain 2001 by Pocket Essentials, 18 Coleswood Road, Harpenden, Herts, AL5 1EQ

Distributed in the USA by Trafalgar Square Publishing, PO Box 257, Howe Hill Road, North Pomfret, Vermont 05053

Copyright © Ashok Banker 2001
Series Editor: Paul Duncan

A CIP catalogue record for this book is available from the British Library.

ISBN 1-903047-45-5

2 4 6 8 10 9 7 5 3

Book typeset by Pdunk
Printed and bound by Cox & Wyman

*This one's for Biki, the spy who loved me
And for Bhagwandas M Luthria, aka Sudhir, for giving me a
Bollywood childhood and playing my 'real-life' father—always
your fan, Pop.*

Acknowledgements

Friends and editors Khalid Mohamed, Ashwin Varde, Kanan Divecha, Nikhil Lakshman and publisher Nari Hira for the columns, the coffee and the career.

David Davidar, to whom I still owe that Bollywood book, and much else.

RK Mehra and all at Rupa & Co.—Here's hoping we can do it again someday.

Rita Mehta and her wonderful staff at *Cine Blitz* for opening up archives and hearts.

And finally Claude Trégoat, whose bright idea this was in the first place, Paul Duncan and Ion Mills.

Cover picture courtesy *Showtime Magazine* (Magna Publishing Co)

CONTENTS

This book is to be returned on or before the
last date stamped below or you will be
charged a fine

New City College – Redbridge campus
Library and Learning Centre
Barley Lane

CONTENTS

CONTENTS

Hindi And Hip:
The Cool New Face Of Bollywood

Check it out. Bollywood, as the Bombay-based Hindi film industry is affectionately nicknamed, is the new cool in international cinema. The world's most prolific film industry has always been regarded with dubious interest by Western critics, film professionals and movie-goers. What else can you expect from a genre that requires every film to have a young good-looking romantic lead couple, half a dozen or more lengthy songs lip-synched by actors to playback singers, costume changes every five minutes and an utter disregard for most film narrative conventions? In spite of these quirky peculiarities—or hell, maybe *because* of them—it has come out of the kitsch closet and taken its place alongside the most respected ethnic films on the planet.

Partly it's a numbers game. India has the fastest population growth rate in the world, the second largest population (over 1.1 billion at the last count) and one of the highest percentages of youth between the ages of 12 and 24. As any Hollywood mogul will tell you over his California champagne, that's the magic age group that fills cinema halls and chews up the movie tickets and popcorn everywhere in the world.

Look at some more figures... In 1985, a staggering 905 feature films were produced in India. This figure was split up into several different ethnic languages, the majority coming out of the Tamil-, Telegu- and Malayalam-speaking states of South India. 185 of the films were in the Hindi language and produced in the sultry Western Indian city of Bombay. It wasn't the peak—that was in 1991 when a record 215 films rolled out of Bombay's overworked processing labs—but it was still a mammoth output.

More than the sheer number of films, it's Bollywood's impact which is immeasurable. If you're used to Hollywood's slick, overproduced product, Hindi films will seem corny, kitsch, even crude at times. On the other hand, if you like music with your movies, the way Australian whizkid Baz Luhrmann did in his spectacular *Romeo+Juliet* and *Moulin Rouge*, you're in for a big treat. In fact, Luhrman flew to Bombay for the release of *Moulin Rouge* where he confessed candidly that the film was inspired by Bollywood.

India has a huge number of expatriate nationals (called Non Resident Indians, or NRIs for short) around the world, mostly based in the USA, UK and Europe. Over the past decade a new generation of educated, fairly well-off, teenage NRIs have shown how fiercely sentimental they are about their Indian origins. Fifty years ago, when film-makers like Raj Kapoor achieved cult status in the then-USSR and Europe, it was considered a bonus. Today, major Bollywood producers like Subhash Ghai and Yash Chopra are producing films aimed primarily at the NRI audience.

Speaking about his most recent release *Yaadein*, Subhash Ghai pointed out that ten years ago, overseas territory accounted for perhaps 10-15% of a film's total earnings, depending on the film. Today, the NRI audience alone brings in 65% of a Bollywood film's total earnings!

Recent hits like *Lagaan* and *Ek Rishta* have earned more from screens in the continental USA and UK than in their home country, despite breaking box-office records locally. It's because the dollar/pound rate is hard to match: an American NRI has 45 times the buying power of an Indian Bollywood buff; a British NRI, 65 times.

Bollywood's main limitations used to be technique and capitalisation. For many years it was forced to depend on shady financiers who charged exorbitant rates of interest—as much as 5% per month or 60% a year compounded—and were often associated with organised crime syndicates. Bollywood was recently given 'industry status,' which means it can avail of bank and institutional loans, and can even float public share issues. A number of professionally-managed companies like Subhash Ghai's Mukta Arts and Pritish Nandy Communications Ltd, to name just two, have successfully raised millions of dollars from public investors and are producing films based on the Hollywood studio model.

The other barrier—technical finesse—has also been overcome. Films like *Gladiator* have successfully outsourced from Bollywood. Remember the statues, pillars, drapes and Connie Nielson's outfits in the film? They all came from Bombay, India! As a spokesperson for Ridley Scott admitted at the time, they did it because they got the same quality at a much, much cheaper price, and faster than they would have in LA or London.

(This isn't just happening with Bollywood. India's computer programming and animation professionals are getting more contracts from Western countries than anywhere else in the world. Every time you dial a toll-free 800 number in the USA, the chances are you will talk to an Indian sitting somewhere in Punjab or Ludhiana, who is glibly affecting a Kansas or Maine accent!)

There's still the budget barrier to consider. Even the biggest Bollywood films are made for around Rs 25-30 crores, or around $5 million. That's because a Bollywood hit can expect to pull in perhaps five times that figure if it's very lucky. With most of the budget spent on superstars who dominate the business in every way imaginable, there's not much left over to make a great movie. This partly explains why Bollywood often doesn't attempt lavish historical costume dramas or CGI-driven monster sagas, although both types of film are loved by Indian audiences. (Dubbed-in-Hindi Hollywood films like *Jurassic Park* and *The Mummy Returns* have raked in as much moolah as a Bollywood hit.) However, with NRI audiences able to spend more on ticket money and the growing number of urban 'class' audiences, both budgets and production values will rise.

Today, there are comparatively few films produced. If you disregard the amateurs who zip in and out, making a film to star their wife's cousin's sister or whatever, you'll probably have less than a couple dozen notable films. Of these, barely ten will earn back their investment. Maybe three or four will make real money. And not one will come close to matching the returns of a Hollywood blockbuster like say, *Pearl Harbour*.

Audiences will forget *Pearl Harbour* by the time the next assembly line, big-studio film rolls out of the well-oiled Hollywood machine. But they won't forget the latest Bollywood hit. Fans go back to watch big Bollywood films a dozen, a hundred, even two hundred times. The stars are mobbed every time they are spotted in public behind their phalanx of armed commando bodyguards. For weeks the songs blare out from every taxi, autorickshaw, Ganpati Pooja mandap and chawl. The Internet buzzes like it did for *The Blair Witch Report*. Even when the next big hit comes along, this one takes its place with all the other great films.

Whatever you do, don't underestimate the power and influence of Bollywood-mania.

India is a country with 17 major languages, almost all of which are spoken by a populace larger than the population of England. It has over 5000 gods, six major religious denominations (Hindu, Muslim, Sikh, Christian, Jain, Buddhist) and ethnic minorities which are the same size as entire Eastern European countries. Yet, if you have to find a single factor that unites the entire nation, it's Bollywood. (Even states like Bengal and Tamil Nadu, where less than 1% of the people speak Hindi, have become major fans of Bollywood.)

If you're wondering why, then maybe it's time you checked out a few of the films in this book. There are theatres running Hindi films in most major cities of the world, and those that you've missed at your multiplex, you can always catch on DVD or VHS. If you're already a Bollywood fan, then you're about to be challenged: Have you seen all the films reviewed and mentioned in this book? Did you realise what made them special the first time around? Chances are, you're going to look at old films in a new light—and vice versa—by the time you've finished reading this little pocket guide.

This little rocket in your pocket is a starter kit designed to launch you into the colourful kitsch world of Bollywood fantasy and melodrama. How high you get is up to you. Just make sure you pack plenty of popcorn, masala flavour.

Silent Screamers

The first Hindi films weren't in Hindi—they were silent movies, silly!
But even so, you can see a distinction between the early Bombay-made
films and those made elsewhere in India. Partly it was that strong Parsi
theatre influence. Partly the leaning toward extravagant symbolism and
Grand Guignol plots. Yup, they were thinking big even then. And then of
course, there were the controversies: nude scenes; off-screen scandals;
the first use of women actors; the 'importing' of Western actors, technicians and (ahem) story ideas. No doubt about it. Long before the word
Bollywood had been coined, Bombay film-makers were already making
their mark on the national cultural scene. The new artistic medium of cinema captured the fancy of the entire nation, but from the very beginning,
it was Bombay that wielded the pioneer's megaphone. Lights! Action!
Chimera!

Raja Harishchandra (1913)

Producer/Director/Writer: DG Phalke (Phalke Films).

Cast: DD Dhabke, PG Sane, Bhalchandra D Phalke, GV Sane, Dattatreya
Kshirsagar, Dattatreya Telang, Ganpat G Shinde, Vishnu Hari Aundhkar, Anna
Salunke, Nath T Telang.

Ishtory: A classic Indian semi-historical legend, derived mostly from
the *Mahabharata*. Raja Harishchandra, a king of the legendary Solar
Dynasty of Ayodhya and an ancestor of Lord Ramachandra, accidentally
violates the sacred space of the seer/sage Vishwamitra. As atonement, the
raja is compelled to renounce his kingdom and endure much hardship
before being forgiven by the Gods. Used to illustrate the Hindu principle
of dharma.

Comment: Although several dozen shorter films had been made earlier, including a number of films of stage plays such as *Pundalik* released
in 1912, *Raja Harishchandra* at 3700 feet (only1475 of which survive
today) is universally acknowledged as the first feature-length Indian film.
Producer/director/writer DG Phalke, later known as Dadasaheb Phalke,
had attended a 1910 screening of the short documentary film *The Life Of
Christ* at PB Mehta's America-India Cinema in Bombay, and was said to
be hugely inspired by the experience. Three years later, Phalke unveiled
his vision of how this exciting new medium could be used to tell a wholly
Indian story. He previewed *Raja Harishchandra* for a small private audience on 2 April 1913 at Bombay's Coronation Cinematograph theatre

and starting commercial screenings the next day. Using a classic Hindu legend was no accident. Phalke, a Maharashtrian Brahmin, was clearly making a subtle anti-colonial statement and an Indian cultural one. Using traditions from the hugely popular and prolific Parsi Theatre movement in Bombay, Phalke shot the film exactly like a stage play for the main part. Tableau in which characters entered and exited from stage/camera left or right, the use of space rather than location changes to depict shifts in setting, the use of untried amateurs (stage performers shied away from the alien medium), the use of male 'actors' for the women's parts (a tradition that would continue for almost two decades longer), and a strict adherence to the stage play script all suggest that Phalke was simply seeking to record and document. Although, in those fledgling days of the medium, simply making a film was a bold experiment. Phalke's pioneering efforts were rewarded with a wave of critical and commercial success, making him the first great legend of Indian cinema, and a forerunner of today's Bollywood. In 1917, Phalke later remade his film in a shorter version titled *Satyawadi Raja Harishchandra*.

Highlights: Unwittingly, the film provides a permanent record of Parsi Theatre of the period, especially the Baliwala Victoria Parsee Theatre group's work. It also documents the spatial choreography of the Sangeet Natak school of Indian classical dancing.

More Like This: Pundalik, Lanka Dahan, Shri Krishna Janma, Sairandhri, Nala Damayanti, Shakuntala.

Kiss-Kitsch Rating: 2/5

Shakuntala (1920)

Producer/Director: Suchet Singh (Oriental Films).

Cast: Dorothy Kingdom, Goharjaan, Sampson, Mrs Sutria.

Ishtory: Based on the classical Sanskrit play by Kalidasa, which retells the legendary romance of Raja Dushyanta and Shakuntala. The rajah, on a hunt in the deep forest, chances upon a beautiful young maiden and falls instantly in love. Later, he exchanges vows and gives her his royal seal ring as proof of his love and commitment to marry. But owing to a curse, after he returns to his kingdom, he loses all memory of her. After waiting and bearing the king's child, Shakuntala travels to his capitol. En route, she loses the ring in a lake and when she faces the king, he fails to recognise her. An old fisherman cuts open a large fish caught from the lake and finds the ring in its belly. He shows it to the rajah, thereby breaking the curse. The king marries Shakuntala, and all ends happily.

Comment: Forget the film. Shakuntala's place in history was assured by the controversy it provoked at the time. Producer/director Suchet Singh committed the grave error of importing Western actors and crew for the film, including the American actress Dorothy Kingdom in the title role and American cameraman Roy Vaughan. While it was commonplace to use Western technicians, even directors, the casting of an American actress in a traditional classic Indian role provoked outrage. A major Videshi-Swadeshi (Western-Indian) debate broke out, spilling over into the newspapers. One producer, SN Patankar, even ran an advertisement in *The Bombay Chronicle* of 24 January 1920 announcing his production of the classic text, to be adapted 'strictly in accordance with the drama.' Another film company, Hindustan Cinema Films, protested the gora (white) casting by proudly claiming that its current release *Usha Swapna* was 'produced by Indian Artistes, by Indian Labour and Without Foreign Assistance.' Clearly, the rising tide of anti-British sentiment had engulfed movie-makers as well. The controversy was further stoked by the immense success of *Shakuntala,* which ran to packed houses for an unusually long 40-day stretch!

Highlights: An American actress playing one of the most traditional of Indian characters—it's sort of like an African American playing Mary, Mother of Jesus, in a 1920 film production!

More Like This: Savitri, Raja Harishchandra.

Kiss-Kitsch Rating: 2/5

Singing In The Train

When Aussie director Baz Luhrmann paid tribute to and deconstructed the Bollywood musical in *Moulin Rouge*, he probably didn't realise that the genre went back almost as far as the period in which his film was set (turn of the 19th century). The musical romance was already a dearly-loved dramatic form in aamchi Mumbai as we Bombay babus call our filmi city. So when the first talking movies rolled out of the studios, they weren't just talking, they came out singing at full throttle. If Garbo had been a Hindi film actress, her historic headline would have read 'Garbo Sings!' However, unlike the classic early American musical *The Jazz Singer*, the first Bollywood musicals weren't just quaint curiosities. Believe it or not, one of them is being remade for the seventh time as this book goes to press!

Alam Ara (1931)

Producer/Director: Ardeshir Irani (Imperial Movietone).

Cast: Master Vithal, Zubeida, Jilloo, Sushila, Prithviraj Kapoor, Elizer, Wazir Mohammed Khan, Jagdish Sethi, LV Prasad.

Ishtory: An ageing rajah is troubled by his two squabbling wives, both of whom wish to bear him an heir. When a fakir (a travelling spiritual man) predicts that one wife will be the lucky one, the other queen tries to seduce the king's general to conspire against the rajah. When the upright general resists her advances, she destroys his family. His daughter Alam Ara survives and is raised by gypsies, who eventually help her invade the palace and expose the vengeful queen's conspiracy. Alam Ara marries the now-grown prince and all ends well.

Comment: India's first 'talkie,' narrowly beating *Shirin Farhad* to the claim, *Alam Ara* was first screened at Bombay's Majestic Theatre on 14 March 1931. Using the mix of song, dance, music and fantasy that would later become the mainstay of the Hindi film genre, it was considered successful enough to be remade twice, in 1956 and 1973, both times by Nanubhai Vakil. *Alam Ara* was based on an original script by popular Parsi playwright Joseph David, who is now best remembered for his scripts for the prolific studio Wadia Movietone (makers of such classic action hits such as *Hunterwali*). Producer/director Ardeshir Irani was an accomplished film-maker with silent hits like *Navalsha Hirji, Mumbai Ni Sethani, Paap No Fej* and *Shahjehan* under his belt. He was far-sighted enough to recognise the historic potential of sound films, and moved

Heaven and earth to make sure his film was the first to be released. Just to be on the safe side, he had posters proclaim: 'India's FIRST Perfect TALKIE.' The same posters also trumpeted (silently, alas): 'All Living, Breathing 100% Talking Peak Drama, Essence of Romance, Brains and Talents Unheard of Under One Banner.' Like its Western counterpart *The Jazz Singer*, *Alam Ara* also had the distinction of featuring the first hit song and established the fact that audiences wanted their movie stars singing and dancing. Eighty years later, things haven't changed much.

Highlights: The first hit film song, 'De de Khuda ke naam pe.' The first film playback singer WM Khan. The title role featured a real-life princess, Zubeida (later India's first woman director), who ironically played a commoner till the end of the film. The Indian Douglas Fairbanks Master Vithal. The first time stage legend Prithviraj Kapoor's famous voice could be heard on film. (Prithviraj Kapoor went on to sire an entire Bollywood dynasty—sons Raj, Shammi and Shashi, grandsons Rishi, Randhir and Rajiv, great-granddaughters Karishma and Kareena Kapoor!)

More Like This: Shirin Farhad, Draupadi, Ayodhya Ka Raja, Indras-abha, Madhuri.

Kiss-Kitsch Rating: 2/5

Hunterwali (1935)

Producer/Director: Homi Wadia (Wadia Movietone).

Cast: Fearless Nadia, Sharifa, Gulshan, Boman Shroff, John Cawas, Master Mohammed, Sayani Atish, Jaidev.

Ishtory: When a princess spurns the advances of her father's prime minister, the villain imprisons the rajah. She assumes the alter ego of the masked Hunterwali (literally the wielder of the 'hunter,' Hindi word for whip) who seeks to redress the wrongdoings and atrocities of the evil usurper. After a bagful of stunts and rousing action set pieces, she is caught bathing naked by a young man whose family was destroyed by the same villain in the name of her father the king. Defeated in a duel and kidnapped by the young man, she manages to convince him to join forces and eventually they triumph over the dastardly villain. Zorro, where the Hell were you when we really needed you?

Comment: Mary Evans, an Australian circus artiste and accomplished ballerina, was known for her live shows performed between film screenings (while the reels were being changed) for British and Indian troops in WWI. While on tour in India, she met Homi Wadia, a fan of Hollywood serial films and Westerns. When Wadia set up his family-owned movie production house, Wadia Movietone, Mary Evans signed on as a chorus girl for their film *Lal-e-Yaman*. Homi Wadia and she were married soon after. Inspired by her gymnastic abilities, her husband envisioned a Pearl White action film series featuring her as the heroine. Renaming her Fearless Nadia, he directed her in her debut, *Hunterwali*, and a legend was born. Hunterwali was the first of a highly-successful action series, usually featuring Fearless Nadia in her customary body-hugging outfits, wielding her trademark whip, riding her trusty steed Punjab Ka Beta (son of Punjab). Mary Evans did her own stunts, some of which were admittedly pretty damn amazing—swinging from building to building, riding her horse over carts and other obstacles, and her legendary 'train-running' stunt in *Miss Frontier Mail* where she ran across the roof of a high-speed train. The train stunt led to a series of train films. The closest to Roy Rogers or John Wayne India ever had, Mary Evans as Fearless Nadia became a sensational female icon, as familiar in her time as Marilyn Monroe in the USA. She was also a great sex symbol—that whip and those tight shirts!—and a shocking reminder that 'women can do it as well.' Not until the emergence of real-life gun-totting legend Phoolan Devi and her immortalisation in Shekhar Kapur's *Bandit Queen* would there be a woman icon to replace Fearless Nadia.

Highlights: Fearless Nadia caught with her pants (and everything else) down in the rare nude-bathing scene. The bhajans (religious chant-songs) by Govind Gopal, including the unlikely one singing the praises of the masked lady champion, 'Hunterwali hai bhali duniya ki sudh leth.' Jaidev, playing Hunterwali's sidekick Chunnoo, later went on to become a noted film composer. *Alam Ara* writer Joseph David's screenplay, based on an original story idea by JBH Wadia, led to his writing virtually every Fearless Nadia film that followed. The whip, the whip, man, the whip! If you're still whimpering for more, check out the 1990 documentary *Fearless: The Hunterwali Story*, produced by Riyad Winci Wadia, grandson of Fearless.

More Like This: Miss Frontier Mail, Hurricane Hansa, Diamond Queen, Jungle Princess, Muqabla, Hunterwali Ki Beti, Flying Prince, Lady Robin Hood, Sher-e-Baghdad, Toofan Queen, Himmatwal, Stunt Queen, Toofani Tirandaz, Chabuk Sawar, Eleven O' Clock, Jungle Goddess, Tigress, Circuswale, Jungle Ka Jawahar, Carnival, Fighting Queen, Jungle Queen, Diler Daku, Circus Queen, Khiladi.

Kiss-Kitsch Rating: 3/5

Devdas (1935)

Producer: New Theatres. Director: PC Barua.

Cast: KL Saigal, Jamuna, KC Dey, Kshetrabala, Rajkumari, AH Shore, Nemo, Biswanath Bhaduri, Ramkumari, Pahadi Sanyal, Kidar Sharma, Bikram Kapoor.

Ishtory: Devdas, son of a zamindar (feudal lord), is a sensitive soul. When he is prevented from marrying his childhood sweetheart Paro, the poor neighbour's daughter, because of their caste/class differences, he is unable to deal with the separation. After Paro is married off to a rich, ageing widower, Devdas is sent away to Calcutta. There he meets and gets involved with a prostitute, gradually sinking into a self-pitying stupor of drink and depression. Finally, he returns home to die in front of his beloved's house.

Comment: Despite its unlikely premise and grim, nihilistic tone, *Devdas* is a key film in Bollywood and Indian history. Before this seminal version by PC Barua, it had been filmed in 1928 by Naresh Mitra. In 1955, it was remade by Barua's cameraman Bimal Roy, who had become an established director in his own right, bringing fame and glory to star Dilip Kumar. It was remade twice in Telegu and was a major influence on Guru Dutt's film oeuvre, especially in films such as *Pyaasa* and *Kaagaz Ke Phool*. Raj Kapoor's character in Ramesh Saigal's *Phir Subah Hogi* is clearly based on *Devdas*. Even the Choti Bahu (daughter-in-law, which is the name by which she is called throughout the film), played by Meena Kumari in Guru Dutt's *Sahib Biwi Aur Ghulam*, is like a female Devdas. These influences are partly explained by the power and effectiveness of the character, as captured in prose by Bengali novelist Saratchandra in his acclaimed novel *Devdas* (he also wrote the novel on which *Sahib Biwi Aur* Ghulam was based, which gives you a hint to that film's similarities). *Devdas* is one of those films that seems to have captured the public imagination in a way that can't easily be explained through intellectual analysis.

Critics have argued that the use of parallel intercutting in the film was the first time the technique had ever been used in such a way: as Devdas falls from his berth in the train, Paro stumbles and falls on the street a thousand miles away. Others have argued that *Devdas* is the sublime creative expression of the Hindu belief in Karma, that it shows how firmly our lives are controlled by destiny, even though we pretend to have free choice. A mythology has sprung up around each and every version of the film, and there are tales of mysterious mishaps during the productions. Even the present-day remake (a mega-budget update starring Shah Rukh

Khan in the title role, under production at time of writing) is plagued by stunt accidents, a bizarre fan incident and its producer being jailed indefinitely. The myth is that it's hard as Hell to make this film but if accomplished, it's sure to be a great success. It has held true for all ten versions so far, so it will be interesting to see if it holds good for the newest remake as well.

Highlights: KL Saigal's stunning Indian classical singing, comparable to the Italian opera style of Pavarotti or his ilk. The songs composed by Rai Chand Boral and Pankaj Mullick were said to have mystical musical mantras imbedded in them—one song was believed to be capable of lighting lamps if sung flawlessly—a feat that Saigal was said to have accomplished during filming! This myth probably sprung up after Saigal's other smash hit *Tansen*. That film had scenes where the title character called down rain, cured people, calmed rioting animals, and caused trees to flower just by singing! Bimal Roy's camerawork was described as 'telepathic' for its ability to communicate the mirrored thought processes of Devdas and Paro. The montage sequence towards the end was one of the longest and certainly the most effective use of the technique in Hindi films. Bengali film-maker and film professor Ritwik Ghatak, considered a guru among film-makers, used *Devdas* to illustrate perfection in cinematography.

More Like This: Devdas (1928), *Tansen*, *Devdas* (1955), *Pyaasa, Kaagaz Ke Phool, Sahib Biwi Aur Ghulam, Phir Subah Hogi, Devdas* (2001).

Kiss-Kitsch Rating: 4/5

Acchut Kanya (1936)

Alternative Title: *The Untouchable Girl*

Producer: Bombay Talkies. Director: Franz Osten.

Cast: Devika Rani, Ashok Kumar, PF Pithawala, Kamta Prasad, Kishori Lal, Kusum Kumari, Pramila, Anwar, Ishrat.

Ishtory: A strange mishmash of Indian caste taboos and an *Anna Karenina*-like tragic drama. A Brahmin boy and a lower caste girl (a scheduled caste, literally 'untouchable') fall in love. In pre-Independence India, their relationship is the ultimate taboo, and ignites a series of violent riots and caste clashes. The girl's father is a railway crossing guard so this inevitably leads to official involvement. Eventually, both lovers are forced to agree to marry partners from their castes, but at the last minute fate intervenes in the form of a tragic train accident.

Comment: Alam Ara took the crown for being the first talkie, but it was *Acchut Kanya* that marked a genuine progression in Hindi films of the 30s. For three decades—since the release of the first Hindi features—the genre had been dominated by mythological melodramas and historical adventures. Flowery dialogue, stagy gestures, cartoonish eye movements carried over from the silent era, and extravagant song sequences with dancing choruses, had become the norm. But none of these daunted Bengali film-maker Himanshu Rai, proprietor of the newly-formed Bombay Talkies, whose wife Devika Rani was one of the biggest stars of the time. Himanshu Rai could barely follow Hindi-Urdu, the language used in movies of that era, so when the script for *Acchut Kanya* came to him it was said he crossed out any line that he couldn't follow. He also dared to cast an unknown Bengali hero in the film, the young Ashok Kumar. (When the leading man on Bombay Talkies' *Jeevan Naiyya* fell ill on the eve of the shoot Kumar, who was working as Rai's lab assistant, was cast instead. In true Bombay Talkies tradition, after he finished shooting for the film, it was back to the lab for young Ashok Kumar, to oversee the editing, mixing and processing of the film.) The result was a film that sounded almost like everyday Hindi, and had natural and unaffected lead performances. Later Ashok Kumar, who went on to become one of Bollywood's greatest stars, reminisced about how terrified he was to act opposite the "dragon lady" Devika Rani, known for her smoking, drinking, cussing and her legendary temper. He also commented that his performance seemed "babyish." Maybe. But hey, he also became a major star after that, earning a princely salary of Rs 300-400 a month. Even though Devika Rani did a total of 14 films in her famous career, it's for this one that she's remembered today. Interestingly, Bombay Talkies employed German director Franz Osten and Austrian cameraman Josef Wirsching. Maybe that accounts for the very phoney depiction of Indian village life in the movie. In typical Bollywood fashion, *Acchut Kanya*'s success made even that phoniness fashionable and set the style for village settings in future films!

Highlights: Ashok Kumar's shy, almost naively innocent performance, which is a striking contrast to the overblown machismo of earlier male action-adventure stars. Ashok Kumar's string of songs in the film: 'Kise kartaa murakh pyar,' 'Pir pir kya kartaa re,' 'Khet ko mooli baagh ko aam' and the smash hit 'Main ban ki chidiya banke ban ban dolun re.' The music composed by Parsi composer, Khursheed Manchershah Minocher-Homji (billed as 'Saraswati Devi' in Bombay Talkies films).

The first major appearance of Mumtaz Ali, mother of future comedic star Mehmood.

More Like This: Jeevan Prabhat, Janmabhoomi, Grama Kanya, Durga, Kangan, Bandhan.

Kiss-Kitsch Rating: 2/5

The Sound Of Masthi

It wouldn't be a Bollywood film without a little, or a lot, of masthi. That's Hindi for mischief, but it's usually used to indicate the joie de vivre spirit of Indians. And nobody displays the spirt of masthi as much as Bombay's bright and brash filmi fraternity. Whether it was Raj Kapoor using Charlie Chaplin as a take-off point for his unique brand of sentimental do-goodery, Ashok Kumar showing how much fun it was to be a bad guy, Dev Anand showing off stylishly, or even the legendary Bimal Roy having a ball behind the camera, Bollywood was showing a fiercely Independent India how to have a great time. Even when it was dealing with life-and-death issues. After all, movies aren't real life. But then again, what is?

Kismet (1943)

Producer: Bombay Talkies. Director: Gyan Mukherjee.

Cast: Ashok Kumar, Mumtaz Shanti, Shah Nawaz, Moti, PF Pithawala, Chandraprabha, VH Desai, Kanu Roy, Jagannath Aurora, Prahlad, Harun, Mubarak, David, Kumari Kamala.

Ishtory: A former theatre owner is haunted by guilt because he crippled his daughter by making her dance to the point of collapse. Impoverished now, father and daughter live on the charity of the theatre's villainous new owner. When a pickpocket befriends the crippled girl's father, love blossoms (with the girl, buddy, not the father). A series of events follows the romance, involving the pickpocket stealing a necklace belonging to the villain's wife, narrowly escaping the cops several times, and finally discovering that he's the bad guy's long-lost son. All's well that ends well, even though the crippled girl still can't dance. But hey, neither can the hero! So it's cool.

Comment: One of the first mega-hits of Hindi cinema, *Kismet* ran for three years without a break at a single theatre in Calcutta. If that doesn't impress you, get outta here. These days, exhibitors complain that even the biggest hits can't pack a houseful audience for more than four weeks. Ashok Kumar, firmly established as the major star of the production studio Bombay Talkies, had overcome his early shy performances and arrived at an enthusiastic zesty style that carries *Kismet* from start to finish. His singing was also effective, despite (or because of?) a persistent smoking habit, and when paired with Mumtaz Shanti, an accomplished singer, he delivered crowd-pleasing hits. The film's melodramatic 'family-divided-family-reunited' plot seems clichéd now but, at the time, it was the first major film to use the device. Later, after Partition (the separation of India and Pakistan into individual nations) cracked countless real families into bits, the theme became ubiquitous. But in *Kismet* it was still used with a touch of innocence and wish-fulfilment, and helped appease the critics. These chaps were outraged by *Kismet*'s bold glamorisation of the criminal life as portrayed by the happy-go-lucky pickpocket hero, and editorials appeared condemning the film for glorifying crime and criminals. In fact, it was this single element, the cheery charming crook played by Ashok Kumar, that was the main reason for the film's success. It was a formula that Navketan Films and the Anand brothers (star Dev Anand and director Vijay Anand) would repeat with similar success in later decades. As it was, producer Mukherjee and his team celebrated their fourth major hit with *Kismet (Kangan, Bandhan* and *Jhoola* being the previous three) and apparently raised enough finance to start their own studio, Filmistan Studio.

Highlights: The curious mixture of realism and comedic style: Shekhar escapes from the cops by vanishing in a puff of cigarette smoke! The patriotic hit 'Aaj himalay ki chot se phir humne lalkara hai.'

More Like This: CID, Victoria 420, Jewel Thief, Johnny Mera Naam.
Kiss-Kitsch Rating: 3/5

Awara (1951)

Alternative Title: *The Tramp*
Producer/Director: Raj Kapoor.
Cast: Raj Kapoor, Nargis, Prithviraj Kapoor, Leela Chitnis, KN Singh, Shashi Kapoor, Cuckoo, Leela Mishra, Baby Zubeida, Honey O'Brien.

Ishtory: Raju, a Chaplinesque Tramp-figure, is bitterly estranged from his high-and-mighty Judge father, partly because of the heartless manner in which the Judge had Raju's mother thrown out of the house. In his oedipal angst, Raju adopts a dacoit (a type of bandit) as his surrogate father, not realising that this is the same man responsible for the misunderstanding that led to his mother being thrown out. When he learns the truth, Raju kills the dacoit and tries to murder his real father as well. He ends up accused of murder in his father's court, defended by his childhood sweetheart. Through his impassioned orations, Raju redeems himself in the eyes of his father and wins the love of the girl, proving that it is possible for even a lower-class vagabond to rise in India's caste-and-class restricted society.

Comment: Perhaps the best-known Hindi film of all time. Even today, *Awara* screenings are still held in remote parts of countries belonging to the former USSR where fans sing along in guttural dialects to those melodious Shankar Jaikishen tunes. And in some places—Greece, for one, and some obscure regions of the Arab nations—the words "Raj Kapoor, Nargis, *Awara*!" are as effective as an entry visa. Working for the first time at his new RK Studio at Chembur, Bombay, built with the profits of his earlier hit *Barsaat*, Raj Kapoor used his family (father Prithviraj, brother Shashi) and his extended professional family of long-time collaborators—composers Shankar-Jaikishen, screenwriters KA Abbas and VP Sathe, lyricists Shailendra and Hasrat Jaipuri, art director Achrekar, cinematographer Radhu Karmakar, and his *Barsaat* co-star Nargis. Conscious of the high expectations of both audiences and critics, Kapoor drove his unit and himself to top the industry standard in every department. The hallucinatory dream sequence alone, added after the film was completed, took three months to shoot! Like Charlie Chaplin's Tramp, Raj Kapoor's Raju persona became an iconic figure in Hindi films, capturing the post-British Raj idealism of the 50s and the common working-class frustration of being unable to bridge the caste/class divide. Later critics would read volumes of intellectual meaning into every detail of the film, trying to crack its Rosebud-like code but, in the end, *Awara* was more than an anti-class statement or a symbolic fantasy. It was the attempt of a star talent, at the peak of his powers, pulling out all the stops to create the tantalising mix of spectacle and emotion that we now call Bollywood. It would be decades before other films would replace *Awara*'s iconic stature. Even today, it remains a nostalgic snapshot of India during those innocent dreamlike post-Independence years.

Highlights: The surrealistic 9-minute-long dream sequence. The climactic prison sequence. The opulent judge's mansion set which would inspire a thousand imitations in real and reel life. Nargis in a swimsuit—the first time a Hindi film heroine had ever appeared in one. Some of the most remembered songs in Hindi film history including 'Awara hoon,' 'Ghar aya mera pardesi' and 'Dum bharke udhar mooh phere, o chanda.'

More Like This: Barsaat, Shri 420, Mera Naam Joker.

Kiss-Kitsch Rating: 5/5

Do Bigha Zameen (1953)

Alternative Title: *Two Acres Of Land*

Producer/Director: Bimal Roy.

Cast: Balraj Sahni, Nirupa Roy, Rattan Kumar, Murad, Jagdeep, Nana Palsikar, Nasir Hussain, Mishra, Dilip Jr., Nandkishore, Rajlakshmi, Tiwari, Noor, Kusum, Hiralal, Sapru, Meena Kumari, Mehmood.

Ishtory: A small Bengali landowner and his son are in danger of losing their two acres of ancestral land unless they repay their debt to the local zamindar (feudal lord). They go to Calcutta to raise the money. The father becomes a rickshaw puller and struggles pitifully against mounting odds. His wife, who joins him in the big city, dies and he suffers a near-fatal accident. Despite his efforts, the ancestral land is taken over and a factory built on the site.

Comment: Bimal Roy, like other Bengali film-makers, was heavily influenced by Vittorio de Sica and the socialist dramas of the Indian IPTA theatre group. Working from a powerful script by Hrishikesh Mukherjee (who also brilliantly edited the film), Roy poured Bengali heart and soul into this sentimental yet moving look at the predicament of the small farmer. Once called the 'backbone of India' by socialist and Marxist ideologists, this sadly-neglected group was being crushed beneath the juggernaut of industrialisation and urbanisation. *Do Bigha Zameen* portrayed the desperate, hopeless plight of these people with a strange combination of high melodrama and neorealism. The neorealism for which it's studied even today was based largely on the performance of Balraj Sahni, who played the landowner-turned-rickshaw puller. An experienced stage actor, Sahni used a naturalistic acting style that was an effective contrast to the melodramatic events assailing him. Director Roy was also commenting subtly on the difference between Bombay's fantasy-oriented cinema and the more gritty, realistic Bengali school of film-making. The shoeshine boy who befriends the son in Calcutta keeps humming the title song from Raj Kapoor's *Awara*, yet no Raj Kapoor blockbuster would ever end so tragically. The shock cuts used by writer-editor Hrishikesh Mukherjee (he claimed to have used the first day-to-night cut in Indian cinema) made the famous rickshaw race sequence as legendary in Indian films as Hitchcock's notorious shower scene. The horrifically implied rickshaw accident at the end of that sequence also helped create an abhorrence for the vehicles that led to their eventual discontinuance. But it's Balraj Sahni's career best performance that makes *Do Bigha Zameen* worth watching today. That, and the sad fact that the protagonist's plight is being repeated even today as tens of millions of rural Indians stream to the cities in search of employment.

Highlights: Balraj Sahni's performance. The joyous sentimentality of the song 'Bhai re, ganga aur jamuna ki dharti kahe pukar ke.' The rickshaw race sequence. Hrishikesh Mukherjee's editing. The exhilaration of the song welcoming the first monsoon in two seasons, 'Hariyala sawan dhol bajata aaya.' Unusually realistic and warm-hearted appearances by future star comedians Jagdeep and Mehmood, and a cameo by sultry siren Meena Kumari.

More Like This: Naya Daur, Mera Gaon Mera Desh, Sahib Biwi Aur Ghulam, Lagaan.

Kiss-Kitsch Rating: 3/5

CID (1956)

Producer: Guru Dutt (Navketan). Director: Raj Khosla.

Cast: Dev Anand, Shakila, Waheeda Rehman, Johnny Walker, Kumkum, KN Singh, Bir Sakhuja, Jagdish, Prabhuji, Uma Devi.

Ishtory: A Bombay police inspector is investigating the murder of a newspaper editor when he meets two women, one the daughter of the police commissioner, the other a mystery lady. The mystery lady tries to bribe him into releasing a criminal from jail. When he refuses, the criminal is killed in prison and he is accused of police brutality. He goes on the run, pursued by the murderer of the editor and his police colleagues, and eventually solves the mystery in a hospital.

Comment: Trained as a classical singer under Pandit Jagannath Prasad, Raj Khosla was 21 and singing at All India Radio when film star Dev Anand spotted him and made him an assistant to star/director Guru Dutt. Dev-saab's legendary ability to spot talent was vindicated when six years later the young assistant directed this smash hit, still acknowledged as one of the first and best modern crime thrillers of Hindi cinema. Heavily influenced by his mentor and producer Guru Dutt's Bombay noir films, director Khosla combined glamour and suspense in a way that hadn't been done before. It had stunningly photographed heroines, sensuously depicted song sequences that continued the story rather than interrupting it, haunting melodic music and an intelligent stylish hero who triumphs by flexing mental muscles rather than physical ones. The intelligent script was by veteran Inder Raj Anand, who took ideas from Hollywood crime films and developed a wholly original screenplay. These elements became part of the Navketan house style.

However, *CID*'s high spots were all outshone by newcomer Waheeda Rehman. This beautiful young actress had already made her debut in a Telegu film down south, and was known for her excellent dancing, but she made her Hindi film debut in *CID* and what a debut! Cinematographer VK Murthy's soft-focus close-ups set a trend that became a hallmark of Waheeda's screen depictions, most unforgettably in producer Guru Dutt's later film *Pyaasa*. From the moment she appears on screen, she steals the show. At times, even camera-hogging hero Dev Anand seems to actually be giving way to her, as if in tribute to her performance and her beauty. And in the famous climactic song sequence 'Kahin pe nigahen' when Waheeda tries to seduce the crime boss to help the hero escape safely, every member of the audience, male and female, was seduced by her pure, flawless sensuality. It was one of the most stunning debuts by a heroine in Hindi films.

CID also became a major launching pad for director Khosla. After an unsuccessful film the previous year, *Milap*, *CID* started him on one of the most legendary careers of any Hindi film director. After working in the Navketan stable for several years, making memorable thrillers and films like *Kala Pani, Bambai Ka Babu* and *Woh Kaun Thi*, he branched off on his own, eventually making his masterpiece *Main Tulsi Teri Aangan Ki*.

Highlights: OP Nayyar's catchy melodies and Majrooh's apt lyrics added glamour to the plot rather than taking away from it. Waheeda's mesmerising screen presence throughout, especially in the soft-focus over-the-shoulder shots. Dev Anand's rakish charm.

More Like This: Baazi, Do Raaste, Who Kaun Thi, Kala Pani, Gupt.
Kiss-Kitsch Rating: 4/5

The Poetry Of Pain

After the rain dance, the rain. And after the euphoria of Independence came disillusionment. Even as Bollywood's self-crowned movie maharajahs began to master the power and majesty of the medium, they also found ways to express their personal anguish and pain. At their worst, they sank into a miasma of melodramatic soap opera. At their best, like the brilliant celluloid portraits of Mehboob and Guru Dutt, they held up a mirror to the entire nation's suffering and cynicism. It was a time of reckoning. And the sultans of kitsch were there to help us find our way through it.

Pyaasa (1957)

Producer/Director: Guru Dutt (Guru Dutt Films).

Cast: Guru Dutt, Waheeda Rehman, Mala Sinha, Johnny Walker, Rehman, Kumkum, Shyam, Leela Mishra.

Ishtory: Vijay, a struggling poet, feels alienated in a post-Independence India besotted with the philistine quest for wealth and comforts. Even his brothers sell off his poems as raddhi (waste paper used for recycling). Only a beautiful prostitute, Gulab (literally Rose) understands his sentiments and loves him and his poetry desperately. But Vijay's heart is with his college sweetheart and she succumbs to the lure of lucre, marrying a rich publisher who represents everything Vijay stands against. When a dead beggar is mistaken for Vijay, the prostitute uses her hard-earned money to pay the publisher to publish a collection of Vijay's poetry. The book is an instant best-seller and critical success. Everyone who earlier dumped on Vijay now gathers to pay tribute to the 'dead' poet. Vijay's appearance at the launch party causes consternation and this elegant gathering watch speechless as he delivers an impassioned song railing against the system. Not surprisingly, he is denounced as a fraud (anything to avoid paying royalties, hey!) and finally renounces the world and walks away with Gulab, heading for unknown destinations.

Comment: Actor/producer/director Guru Dutt came out of nowhere. His tragic epics have no predecessor in either Hindi or Western films. His vision was wholly unique. His genius unmistakable. The only comparisons that do justice would be to film-makers like Satyajit Ray, Ritwik Ghatak or perhaps the young Orson Welles. *Pyaasa* was the first of four great films that explored Guru Dutt's favourite theme: the place of the artist in a crassly commercial world. The other three films were *Kaagaz*

Ke Phool, Chaudvin Ka Chand and *Sahib Biwi Aur Ghulam. Pyaasa* remains the purest expression of his basic theme. It is no coincidence that his character's name, Vijay, would go on to become the most favoured character name in Bollywood, acquiring a mythology of its own. The name literally means Victory and where Amitabh Bachchan and his collaborators would later use it to mean a violent and cathartic victory over crime and corruption, Guru Dutt used it in its most philosophical sense. Coming from the Navketan tradition of noirish thrillers and musical romances (he was uncle to the Anand brothers Dev and Vijay), Guru Dutt had already made the cash registers and critics sing out with his thoroughly enjoyable entertainers like *Baazi, Aar Paar* and *Mr & Mrs '55*. *Pyaasa* came as a complete shock to the system. The brooding imagery of the black and white photography, the tragic tone undercut with gauche comedic asides, the poetic sensuality of his heroine, the unrelenting bleakness of his world-view and his painfully honest look of post-Independent Indian reality, all made for a powerful cocktail. The public drank it all up, underwriting Guru Dutt's vision and honesty. There is an essential sense of desolation in the Indian psyche, an almost Hindu awareness that things mostly don't work out and often go bad real easily. It's this same soul sadness that makes us love ghazals—the Indian semi-classical equivalent of 'somebody done somebody wrong' Country & Western moaners. It's no coincidence that Guru Dutt's character appears unshaven and dishevelled throughout *Pyaasa*, or that the haunting songs are like modern-day ghazals. *Pyaasa* is the ultimate 'nobody cares' sad song on celluloid, threatening to drown in artistic self pity at any moment. It's only Guru Dutt's considerable mastery over the film medium that elevates it to the level of art. His use of the Christ-on-the-cross posture is subtle to the point of being subliminal, yet is repeated throughout the film and his oeuvre. His unconventional unheroic looks make his achievement even more remarkable. This is a film about a real person, not a film star attempting to pass off as one. In today's fresh-face-and-beautiful-buns obsessed Bollywood, there would be no place for Guru Dutt. Then again, he would rather be dead than be here. On the other hand, he would be very pleased to know that his work is still regarded as a triumph of the Hindi film form. In the end, he did have his Vijay.

Highlights: Waheeda Rehman, photographed as only a Guru Dutt heroine could be (check out Meena Kumari in his *Sahib Biwi Aur Ghulam* too). Guru Dutt's brooding introspective tour-de-force performance—and to think that he almost cast Dilip Kumar in the role! Writer Abrar Alvi's picture-perfect screenplay and glowing Urdu dialogues, based on

Saratchandra's story *Srikanta*. Lyricist Sahir's bitterly cynical words and SD Burman's almost unplugged compositions: 'Jaane who kaise log the jinko,' 'Yeh mahalon yeh takhton,' 'Aaj sajan mohe ang lagalo,' 'Jinhe naaz hai hind par who kahan hain' and the pièce de résistance 'Jala do yeh duniya.'

More Like This: Devdas, Kaagaz Ke Phool, Chaudvin Ka Chand, Sahib Biwi Aur Ghulam.

Kiss-Kitsch Rating: 5/5

Mother India (1957)

Producer/Director: Mehboob Khan (Mehboob Productions).

Cast: Nargis, Sunil Dutt, Raaj Kumar, Rajendra Kumar, Kanhaiyalal, Jilloo, Kumkum, Master Sajid, Sitara Devi.

Ishtory: A farmer loses both arms in an accident and abandons his family rather than face the humiliation of being unable to support them. His wife is faced with the task of farming the land while raising two young sons during a period of great struggle for Indian farmers. She toils magnificently, performing great sacrifices to raise her sons, including selling her body to the village moneylender to buy them food. When they're grown, one son becomes a rebel, taking to the gun rather than struggling like his mother and dutiful brother have done. In the most famous ending of any Hindi film, the mother shoots her son, performing the final act of motherly resonsibility in this epic saga of motherhood.

Comment: Mother India has been called the Indian *Gone With The Wind* for obvious reasons. Like the 1939 American Civil War epic, it depicts the end of a dream, the painful struggle of the idyllic rural Indian farmer to cling to the glory of bygone days. The female protagonist is as tenacious and determined as Scarlett O'Hara, except that her goal is to stand her sons on their own feet. But there the similarities end sharply. *Mother India* is a triumph of the Hindi film rhetorical style over Western narrative pace. Through a symbolic yet dramatic screenplay, the film unfolds its message of Indian motherhood and Maa shakti (Mother power), which inspired countless films from *Deewar* to *Ganga Jamuna* while tapping into the Indian male's obsessive adoration of his mother figure. At its starkest level, *Mother India* is a powerful vindication of women's empowerment. At a more symbolic level, it's a nationalist state-ment on the strength and tenacity of the Indian character, able to with-stand epic struggles and strife. It's a powerful tale of a mother and two sons—one dutiful and law-abiding, the other rebellious and defiant—and their highly Oedipal, tempestuous relationship. Interestingly, Nargis had become a mainstay of Raj Kapoor's RK production banner, refusing all outside offers for several years. The reason was believed to be at least partly due to her alleged romantic attachment to Raj Kapoor. This changed dramatically when she accepted Mehboob Khan's offer to play a woman twice her age (she had previously turned down Raj Kapoor's request to play an older woman in another untitled film). During the making of *Mother India*, she was rescued during an on-set fire by her screen son Sunil Dutt, with whom she then had an affair (maybe that accounts for some of the Oedipal overtones in the film!) which culminated in their marriage.

Highlights: Nargis in the greatest female role in Bollywood history. Sunil Dutt's passionately wild and rebellious performance. Rajendra Kumar's true-to-type good-boy part. Raaj Kumar's small but effective cameo as the father. Kanhaiyalal's lecherous and disgusting moneylender was so effective that he was said to be spat on and abused by the film's fans after its release!

More Like This: Aurat, Son Of India, Deewar, Gunga Jamuna.
Kiss-Kitsch Rating: 4/5

Madhumati (1958)

Producer/Director: Bimal Roy (Bimal Roy Productions).

Cast: Dilip Kumar, Vyjayanthimala, Johnny Walker, Pran, Jayant, Tiwari, Misra, Baij Sharma, Bhudo Advani, Jagdish, Sagar, Ranjeet Sud, Sheojibhai, Tarun Bose.

Ishtory: A traveller takes shelter from a storm in a decrepit deserted mansion where he sees a portrait of the late owner, a raja. The portrait triggers off memories of his past life (cue for flashback) when he was a a foreman on the raja's plantation. In that past life, he fell in love with a tribal woman. Their romance came to an end when the raja began to lust after the same woman and she died trying to escape his clutches. In classic Hindi reincarnation-film fashion, the lovers each swore they would be reunited, "even if I have to be reborn a thousand times." (End flashback.) The hero finds another woman who is the spitting image of his former-life lover. Their romance begins anew, and this time they resolve to take revenge on the raja—who, amazingly, is still alive, spry and libidinous! In the end, the dead tribal woman returns from the dead to do the grisely deed herself, blesses both present-day lovers whose cycle of rebirth is presumably over at last.

Comment: Madhumati is widely regarded as the most effective supernatural thriller ever made in India. It's also one of those rarities—a box-office smash that's critically acclaimed as a masterpiece of film-making. The film combined a number of elements in a manner that had never been attempted before, let alone achieved so effectively. The haunting B&W spookiness, the spine-tingling music score, the depiction of tribal imagery and customs, the songs which seem to add immensely to the atmosphere and characters rather than detract from them, the reincarnation plot, and the final, unexpected supernatural twist at the climax have all been much imitated since with little success. Somehow, everything came together perfectly for *Madhumati*, making it unique in the history of Hindi cinema.

It all began with a brilliantly-realised script written by Ritwik Ghatak, the great alcoholic art film director whose films barely got an audience in his lifetime but are now revered by film students and critics. Ghatak had just come off making *Ajantrik (1957)*, a film set against a tribal background. In it he had captured the alienness of Indian tribesmen, many of whom still live like their ancestors did five thousand years ago, with an authenticity that gave the film a genuinely 'different' feel.

Director Bimal Roy could easily have turned *Madhumati* into another Bengali art film. Instead, he chose to make it as an unabashedly commercial Bollywood flick and history was created.

Highlights: Lata Mangeshkar's classic ditty, 'Aaja re pardesi.' Ritwik Ghatak's story and screenplay. Rajinder Singh's dialogue. Salil Choudhury's background score and song compositions. Hrishikesh Mukherjee's editing. Pran's performance as the raja.

More Like This: Mehbooba, Mahal, Kudrat, Hamesha.

Kiss-Kitsch Rating: 5/5

Kaagaz Ke Phool (1959)

Producer/Director: Guru Dutt (Guru Dutt Films).

Cast: Guru Dutt, Waheeda Rehman, Baby Naaz, Johnny Walker, Mahesh Kaul, Veena, Minoo Mumtaz, Pratima Devi.

Ishtory: A brilliant Hindi film director loses his wife and infant daughter because of the disreputibility of his profession. He discovers and falls in love with a young woman, who becomes the star of his most successful films. After her premature retirement from films, he falls into a spiral of depression and alcoholism, eventually ending up as an impoverished extra in the same studio where he once called the shots. The return of his heroine changes his fortunes once more, but comes too late to save him from his self-destruction. Finally, he is found dead in a director's chair in an empty film studio.

Comment: If *Pyaasa* was about the thirst for great art, *Kaagaz Ke Phool* is about slaking that thirst, and discovering that it was an illusion all along. You can never satisfy your inner thirst for greatness, because artistic genius contains the seeds of its own destruction. If this strikes you as a fit subject for a great film, you're in luck because *Kaagaz Ke Phool* is one of the most brilliantly realised artistic visions in Hindi cinema. Perhaps too brilliant—the film was a box-office disaster. As Guru Dutt admitted in a famous and much-quoted essay 'Classics And Cash,' he wrote it was 'good in patches... too slow... and it went over the head of audiences.' In a less charitable paragraph, he also wrote that making a great Hindi film was like 'an angel beating his wings in a void,' quoting Matthew Arnold's description of the tragic life of Shelley. *Kaagaz Ke Phool* was India's first Cinemascope film, and both cinematographer VK Murthy and producer/director Guru Dutt shot some of the most breathtaking B&W sequences and images ever seen in Hindi cinema. This vision was so fully realised, it was too much for mass audiences to absorb in the same way that some of Orson Welles' work was too rich for American film-goer's blood. It was also one of the few films set against the backdrop of Bollywood, a notoriously jinxed subject. For some reason, Hindi film audiences seem unable to accept films that go behind the scenes of their favourite fantasy factory. Perhaps because it dispels the fantasy. In a country where a surprising percentage of film-goers still believe that film stars really are the characters they play on screen, and that they sing and speak the playback songs and scripted dialogue entirely under their own steam, it's hard to get them to take a brutal, realistic and ultimately tragic look at the grime beneath the glamour. But for those who are interested, Guru Dutt put it on celluloid for all eternity, capturing a sense of epic romantic and artistic tragedy that is more than the sum of the film's parts. Even today, individual elements—a song, an image, a line of dialogue—remain imbedded in the national consciousness, in much the same way that snatches of Raj Kapoor's equally self-indulgent *Mera Naam Joker* are recalled fondly. But where Raj Kapoor used his considerable skills to create a curious mishmash, Guru Dutt created a genuine masterpiece. To hell with what the box office said.

Highlights: VK Murthy's Oscar-worthy cinematography, the first use of Cinemascope in India, has imagery that gives the film an epic dimension. It shows, not tells, the inherent theme of artistic brilliance and the

32

loneliness of genius. Writer Abrar Alvi's powerfully poetic Urdu dialogue (Guru Dutt is said to have collaborated on the dialogue, uncredited). Kaifi Azmi's soul-stirring lyrics, especially 'Waqt ne kiya' (perhaps the single greatest Hindi film song ever written) and 'Dekhi zamaane ki yaari,' are ably matched by SD Burman's haunting melodies. Waheeda Rehman's luminous beauty and performance—clearly based on her off-screen relationship with Guru Dutt. The depiction of the Hindi film industry of the 1950s, which was still a disreputable profession that was equated to prostitution and gambling.

More Like This: Devdas, Pyaasa, Sahib Biwi Aur Ghulam, Khamoshi, Abhimaan.

Kiss-Kitsch Rating: 5/5

Last Dance

Time to hang up those dancing shoes. Hollywood bade goodbye to its cowboys and tap dancers soon after World War II brought reality crashing through the cardboard fantasy backdrops. Bollywood didn't play the retreat quite so quickly or decisively. Instead, it played a variety of notes on that gleaming gold trumpet at sunset, attempting to see whether film could capture the new maturing mood of India. A film without songs, a love triangle that focussed more on the sexual undertones than the superficiality of songs and dances, a grim classic documenting the end of an era and the start of a new age, a patriotic drama that borrowed freely from the Government propaganda line, and perhaps the last great historical costume drama produced on those crumbling Bombay sound stages. An old order was ending, and a new order was struggling to find its place. But there was always time for a song and a dance, and another, and another, and...

Mughal-e-Azam (1960)

Producer/Director: K Asif (Sterling Investment Corp.).

Cast: Prithviraj Kapoor, Dilip Kumar, Madhubala, Durga Khote, Nigar Sultana, Ajit, Kumar, Murad, Jilloo, Vijayalakshmi, S Nazir, Surendra, Gopi Krishna, Jalal Agha, Baby Tabassum, Johnny Walker.

Ishtory: The legendary love story of Mughal Emperor Akbar's son Salim and his doomed affair with a slave girl. Salim, a playboyish prince, receives a nude statuette as a gift for winning a battle. He falls in love with the effigy, and then with the girl, Anarkali. The emperor, outraged by his son's involvement with a slave, warns Salim to let her go. But Salim, obsessed with his love for Anarkali, defies his father and challenges him to battle. The emperor defeats his only son and condemns him to death for rebelling against him. In the original legend, the story ended with Akbar condemning Anarkali to death as well, by having her walled in alive, but *Mughal-e-Azam* ends with the Emperor sparing Anarkali's life without Salim's knowledge.

Comment: The historical drama had always been a favourite staple of Indian films in general, and Hindi films in particular. Many believe that the genre peaked with this classic spectacular. K Asif, known for his historical films centred around Muslim legends, like *Phool, Hulchul* and *Love And God,* poured nine years of effort into making *Mughal-e-Azam* (17 years, if you count development time and the raising of finance). The

34

delay was partly due to the project's daunting budget and production challenges. The first major hitch was the death of Chandramohan, a superstar who had acted in Sohrab Modi's *Pukar* and Mehboob's *Humayun*. His second pick, Dilip Kumar, proved to be the perfect choice. Dilip Kumar's classic features and low-key style were just what the role needed, while the film proved to be his most famous part. The other two major roles, played by Prithviraj Kapoor and Madhubala, also proved perfect. (Rumours were rife about an on-set romance between Dilip Kumar and Madhubala.) Asif's problems had only begun. Taking an inordinately long time to get things just right, the perfectionist discovered that he had gone over budget halfway through the film. He trudged on determinedly, borrowing money from the 'market' at exorbitant rates of interest. His ambition was to make a film that would be remembered for generations. He was vindicated when the completed film sold to distributors for the unheard-of price of Rs 17 lakhs per territory, at a time when most films fetched Rs 3 or 4 lakhs per territory. The film was among the first to use colour in part—for the famous Sheesh Mahal (Palace of Mirrors) sequence. The epic camerawork and staging that Asif took so much care and time getting just right were impressive, yet they were overshadowed by the powerful confrontation scenes between the emperor and his son, for which the film is best remembered today. It marks the best of the classical style of film-making, soon to give way to a more casual, modern approach with the social family dramas of the 1960s. Ironically, K Asif made only four films in his life, and three of his leading men died before completing the films!

Highlights: Dilip Kumar and Madhubala's teasing romantic scenes, especially the feather-tickling scene, later called 'the most erotic scene in Hindi films.' Prithviraj Kapoor's imposing emperor, with his legendary booming dialogue delivery—tragically, he lost the use of his famous voice a few years later. Dilip Kumar and Prithviraj Kapoor's scenes together. The classical Urdu dialogue by Kamal Amrohi, Ehsan Rizvi and Wajahat Mirza. Madhubala's coy performance and nasal singing voice. RD Mathur's camerawork, slow, stately and epic. Naushad's famous score, especially the evergreen 'Pyar kiya to darna kya hai.' Classical maestro Bade Ghulam Ali Khan's 'Shubh din aaye' and 'Prem jogan ban ke chali.'

More Like This: Anarkali, Rustom, Sheesh Mahal, Jhansi Ki Rani, Humayun, Mother India, Razia Sultan.

Kiss-Kitsch Rating: 3/5

Kanoon (1960)

Producer/Director: BR Chopra (BR Films).

Cast: Ashok Kumar, Rajendra Kumar, Nanda, Nana Palsikar, Mehmood, Om Prakash.

Ishtory: A Hindi film without songs. Isn't that enough? Nope, you want a story too? Okay, here it comes: A liberal judge's daughter marries a broad-minded public prosecutor. The prosecutor's mind is further broadened when he witnesses his pa-in-law commit murder (liberally, we assume). When a petty thief is wrongly arrested for the crime and tried in the judge's court, the son-in-law decides he's had enough. He steps forward and has his pa-in-law arrested (goodbye, anniversary gifts). That's when our hero learns that the killer wasn't the judge after all, but an identical lookalike. In keeping with the film's overall unconventionality (no songs!), all this is used to further an impassioned speech against (gasp) capital punishment. Moral of the story: Don't tell on the in-laws.

Comment: Baldev Raj Chopra, or BR Chopra as he's known, was an émigré from Lahore who came to India after the country's partition with Pakistan. Although he had some film experience and was a great fan of Hollywood's brooding films noirs, he was a journalist by profession. Not your typical Bombay-bred made-in-Bollywood product at all. He adjusted to the musical narrative of commercial Hindi films quickly, finding success with hits like *Afsana, Chandni Chowk* and *Naya Daur*, but with *Kanoon* he took on the greatest risk of his career. The idea of a film without songs may seem commonplace anywhere else in the world, but in the industry it was unimaginable then and even remains unthinkable today. BR Chopra shocked the pundits by not only making a long (two and half hours) movie without songs, but by making a box-office hit! Seen today, *Kanoon* seems overly talky, a couple of the plot twists seem contrived, and the obvious tributes to film noir style in the brooding B&W camerawork look dated. But the film works as a suspense thriller, breaking new ground in its portrayal of an unusual family tangle against the background of the legal profession. Chopra's experience as a journalist has been credited for his realistic approach. Although the courtroom drama was an established genre in Hindi films, *Kanoon* was one of the few films to depict the profession of law. And believe me, it's a relief not to hear the lawyers break into song and dance every time they're out of the courtroom! Why didn't *Kanoon*'s financial and critical success inspire other film-makers to cut the songs out of their films? Nobody knows for sure, but perhaps the fact that it took an outsider with a non-film background to attempt this seemingly obvious innovation may answer that question. To every Bollywood-bred director, it was probably an intimidating breakthrough and too tough an act to follow.

Highlights: No songs. Cinematographer MN Malhotra's effective crane and trolley/dolly takes. Writer Akhtar-ul-Iman's verbose but effective dialogue. Ashok Kumar's tour-de-force performance. Director BR Chopra's ability to keep the suspense taut despite a general lack of relief. And most of all, no songs!

More Like This: Go out there and make some, please!

Kiss-Kitsch Rating: 3/5

Sahib Biwi Aur Ghulam (1962)

Producer: Guru Dutt (Guru Dutt Films). Director: Abrar Alvi (Guru Dutt is believed to have co-directed).

Cast: Meena Kumari, Guru Dutt, Waheeda Rehman, Rehman, Nasir Hussain, Sapru, Sajjan, SN Bannerjee, Dhumal, Krishan Dhawan.

Ishtory: An educated but low-class man arrives in 19th-century British-run Calcutta seeking work. He witnesses the British looting stores and observes the general decay of the old feudal system as a new order comes into being. He gets a job at a factory and accommodation at an old haveli (mansion). The owners of the haveli are a decadent zamindar family fallen on hard times. The bride of the youngest son attracts the attention of our hero. While her husband dallies with dancing girls and squanders the last of his family fortune in all-night booze binges, his wife seeks solace in alcohol and sad songs. Drawn to this tragic self-destructive woman, the young tenant soon falls into an obsessive platonic relationship with her. He is forced to leave the house when their platonic friendship threatens to get physical, and believes he is doing the honourable thing. But her brother-in-law has already assumed her infidelity and has paid some ruffians to murder her for sullying the family honour. Years later, he returns to the now-abandoned haveli and finds her skeleton in the remains. Only then does he find out that she was murdered.

Comment: After the failure of his magnificent *Kaagaz Ke Phool*, Guru Dutt was as soul-sick as his character in *Pyaasa*. He was disgusted enough to want to quit films but financial compulsions forced him to continue. Still, he refused to direct *Chaudvi Ka Chand* and when it became a smash hit, descended even deeper into alcohol and depression, not unlike his character in *Kaagaz Ke Phool*. By the time he made *Sahib Biwi Aur Ghulam* he refused to act as well. But the role was turned down by his first choice, Shashi Kapoor, and even lesser star Biswajeet refused to take on the risky role. Forced to play the part himself, Guru Dutt hired writer Abrar Alvi to helm the film, although allegations of Dutt ghost-directing abide to the present day. He faced problems in the other casting too: Nargis, his first choice for the small but pivotal role of the alcoholic abandoned wife, refused, allegedly because Dutt had previously dropped her husband, film star Sunil Dutt, from his earlier film *Raaz*. His personal life was also in shambles. His long, highly-publicised affair with co-star Waheeda Rehman had wrecked his marriage to singer/star Geeta Dutt who refused to sing playback for Waheeda Rehman in this film. By the time the film was over, so were both his affair and marriage. The story goes that he tried at least twice to commit suicide during the making of this—he eventually succeeded in his attempts two years later. As if all this wasn't enough, the heroine he eventually cast, Meena Kumari, was an alcoholic as was Dutt. (She died several years, men and bottles later, in a gruesome physical breakdown caused by alcohol.) But if you put all this macabre backstory aside and watch *Sahib Biwi Aur Ghulam* for its merits, you'll be treated to one of the classics of Hindi cinema, and certainly Guru Dutt's greatest achievement. Dutt returned to his roots for this one, drawing heavily from Bengali literature and film for inspiration. Basing the story on Bimal Mitra's Bengali novel *Saheb Bibi Golam*, Dutt turned it into a tragic record of the end of the Indian feudal era and the start of the new, apparently British/Westernised age, in turn-of-the-19th-century Calcutta. This changing of the guard is clearly illustrated by the film's opening sequences and the hero working by day in a modern city factory while staying by night in the decaying old-world mansion. Throughout, images of modernism and snatches of history pervade the intensely personal, baroque world of the zamindar family, who stubbornly cling to the trappings of the old order. The hero's intrusion into the household, triggering a chain of events that hasten the family's imminent ruin, is amplified by his modern education and lower-class background. The Choti Bahu (daughter-in-law) with whom he becomes obsessed is clearly symbolic of the old way of life, self-destructing in the face of modern urbanism. *Sahib Biwi Aur Ghulam* was the first Hindi film to openly deal with the issue of a woman's sexual dissatisfaction—the Choti Bahu confronts her husband and accuses him of neglecting her needs in a scene that shocked audiences. The mood throughout is dark, but by the end it descends into a morbid morass that is almost hypnotically watchable. Meena Kumari's sexually-frustrated, alcohol-immersed character is one of the greatest female characters ever portrayed on the Hindi film screen. The small touches of irony throughout—the hero works by day in a factory that manufactures sindoor (the red ochre powder used by Indian wives to indicate their marital status) and slips closer to infidelity with a married woman by night—and the relentless darkness of the narrative make *Sahib Biwi Aur Ghulam* unmissable by any fan of classic Hindi cinema.

Highlights: Novelist Bimal Mitra's story and director/scriptwriter Abrar Alvi's script capture a world and a time never seen before, except briefly in Satyajit Ray's *Jalsaghar*. Meena Kumari's performance, no doubt inspired by her self-obsessed tragic real-life history. Cameraman VK Murthy's dark camerawork that progresses deeper into shadows and depression as the story darkens. Producer/star Guru Dutt's pitch-perfect performance as the young innocent confronted by baroque decadence. Waheeda Rehman's butterfly-bright presence in this otherwise dark prison of a movie. Composer/singer Hemant Kumar's (aka Hemant Mukherjee) career best music score, including the classic songs 'Na jao saiyan chhodke,' 'Bhanwra bada nadan' and 'Saakiya aaj mujhe neend.'

More Like This: Jalsaghar (Bengali), *Pyaasa, Kaagaz Ke Phool*.

Kiss-Kitsch Rating: 5/5

Sangam (1964)

Alternative Title: *The Confluence*

Producer/Director: Raj Kapoor (RK Films).

Cast: Raj Kapoor, Vyjayanthimala, Rajendra Kumar, Lalita Pawar, Achala Sachdev, Iftikhar, Nana Palsikar, Raj Mehra.

Ishtory: A lower-class boy's best friends are an upper-class boy and girl. As the three grow up, both boys vie for the girl's love in a classic Hindi film love triangle. The poor boy overcomes his class disadvantage by joining the Air Force and becoming a national hero. He gets the girl, Radha, marries her, and should spend the rest of his life happily ever after. But he's terribly insecure and fears his wife might be unfaithful to him—she still enjoys the company of her high-society acquaintances. Obsessed by his uneasy fantasies, he's unable to establish a normal conjugal relationship. Finally, his friend, who still loves the woman but has tried hard not to show it, realises that he's the thorn in the side of their marriage and commits suicide, sacrificing himself for the happiness of his friends. Before he dies, he assures the jealous husband that he has never laid hands on his wife and that she is as pure as the driven snow. The hero regrets his jealousy and realises too late that his friendship was worth far more than his marriage, but tragically, it's too late.

Comment: As always, Raj Kapoor's fascination with sexuality came through clearly despite the strict moral code of Hindi cinema. In this, his first colour film, he played with phrases, words, situations and imagery to create a sense of sexual tension that would have been absent had any other director or producer helmed this script. The title, referring to the point at which both the sacred rivers Ganga and Jamuna reach a confluence, is a not-so-subtle metaphor for sexual joining. This is underlined in the title song, rendered by Raj Kapoor playing a set of bagpipes on the branch of a tree as he pleads with Radha bathing in a swimsuit in the river below, begging her to "join" her river with his. On their honeymoon in Paris—the location again chosen for its sexual-romantic association—it's implied that he's temporarily impotent or simply unaroused. Radha promptly acts like a prostitute, crooning a song that taunts his lack of arousal—literally, "What can I do, O Rama, I've gone and married an old man!" Even watching the film today, the charged sexuality of every scene comes through sharply, as does the class difference between the hero and heroine. As for the sexual anxiety and fear of infidelity, this real-life problem in Indian couples was common enough for director Raj Kapoor to insert an impassioned speech by the distraught Radha pleading for better treatment of women. In contrast to the on/off sexuality of the heterosexual couple, the relationship between the two male friends verges on the classic. This isn't just a story device—it accurately reflects the classic Indian male camaraderie in a country where it's common for completely heterosexual male friends to walk hand in hand in public and pledge to sacrifice their lives for one another. The subtle underlying message, recycled in any number of lesser films, is that a male/female sexual relationship can never match the trust and surety of a male/male sex-free bonding. Critics have since commented at length on various aspects of *Sangam*'s sexual undertones, but it's also possible to watch it as a simple love triangle tale.

Highlights: The location photography in exotic European backdrops like snowy Switzerland and sultry Paris—*Sangam* was the first film to use such foreign locales so glamorously (in colour). Shankar-Jaikishen's music score, including the hit songs 'Ye mera prem patra,' 'Bol Radha bol sangam,' and 'Main kya karoo Ram.' Raj Kapoor's deferential, nervous anxiety, is as if his trademark Raju persona is entering a new world of mature relationships and upper-class expectations. Vyjayanthimala's teasing pointy-bra playfulness, rendered in the almost mimelike acting style of the age, perfectly mirrors the over-affected femininity of those years. She's not Marilyn, but she's not bad either!

More Like This: Pyasa, Saajan, Sagar, Hum Dil De Chuke Sanam.
Kiss-Kitsch Rating: 3/5

Waqt (1965)

Producer: BR Chopra (BR Films). Director: Yash Chopra.

Cast: Sunil Dutt, Raaj Kumar, Sadhana, Sharmila Tagore, Shashi Kapoor, Balraj Sahni, Shashikala, Motilal, Rehman, Achala Sachdev, Madan Puri, Jeevan.

Ishtory: An earthquake splits a family apart. Tracing his children, the father learns that one of his sons was physically abused by the warden of an orphanage. The father kills the warden and is sentenced to 20 years in prison. The son is raised a criminal to become a slick burglar, while his brothers become a lawyer and a poor chauffeur. All three brothers fall for the same woman and fall out with each other. But when the burglar is framed for a murder, brother lawyer comes to his rescue and defends him in court, while brother chauffeur does his bit to clear his brother's name. All this without knowing they're brothers!

Comment: Waqt was a major commercial hit. This may partly justify some of its more kitsch melodramatic elements. In fact, it set the tone for several future mega-hits reusing old film devices in updated ways. The 'brothers separated in childhood' device is used effectively, with strong casting making the career choices believable. Raaj Kumar, the gravelly throated, affected stylist, makes a fascinating master thief. Sunil Dutt's boisterous enthusiasm makes him a great playboy. The film also portrayed the luxurious, deliciously decadent lifestyles of Bombay's rich kids for the first time in Hindi films. This nouveau riche class was the first batch of post-Independence babies coming of age in an India where 99% were starting to starve while a fraction of a percent were getting filthy rich from every carpet-bagging deal imaginable. Producer BR Chopra (big brother of director Yash Chopra) was fond of the Hollywood Golden Age system of film-making: He couldn't quite manage to get stars to work on a weekly salary, but he did try to effect start-to-finish shooting schedules. He managed this the same way the Hollywood studios managed to churn out films by the fortnight—by shooting extensively on sets. To capture the opulent lifestyle of Bombay's Pali Hill brat pack on sound stages, he virtually invented a kitsch art direction that worked in a peculiar, stylised way: Pink walls, blue walls, fountains in bedrooms, circular beds, mirrored ceilings. And all the toys that India's masses had never even heard about let alone seen with their own eyes before: low-slung sports cars, motor boats, uniformed chauffeurs, housemaids, gold watches. Less than ten years later, brother Yash Chopra would contribute in a large way to dismantling the glamour of these same pop artefacts by relegating them to the villains of his films, smugglers and dirty dealers, and such extravagances became instant shortcut-images of ill-gotten gains in any Bollywood film. So much so, that it was considered anathema to have any film's hero from a rich background or have any of the status symbols. However, back in the sweet 60s it was still possible for the two-anna film-going masses to fantasise about owning such things through honest labour. This kitsch innocence dates *Waqt* irreparably, making it a quaint curiosity marked by strong acting and a peculiar blend of melodrama and stylised realism that were uniquely BR Chopra's trademarks. It would take the young brother a few more years and several more films to put his own trademark stamp on his films.

Highlights: The star turns, especially the unusual clash of personalities between Raaj Kumar and Sunil Dutt. The art direction and colour scheme. The hit score by relatively unknown music director Ravi. Asha Bhosle's memorable renditions of 'Din hair bahar ke' (with Mahendra Kapoor) and the haunting solo number 'Aage bhi jaane na tu.' The hit song sung by Manna Dey 'Ai meri zohrajabeen,' the first of many hundreds of such boy-harasses-girl songs to come in Bollywood films.

More Like This: Kismet, Awara, Amar Akbar Anthony, Naseebl.
Kiss-Kitsch Rating: 2/5

Teesri Manzil (1966)

Director: Vijay Anand.

Cast: Shammi Kapoor, Asha Parekh, Premnath, Helen, KN Singh, Raj Mehra, Prem Chopra, Laxmi Chhaya, Neeta, Sabina, Salim, Rashid Khan.

Ishtory: A young woman, Sunita, gets news that her sister has committed suicide in a tourist hill town. Apparently, she was distraught after being rejected by her lover, a drummer in a hotel jazz band. Sunita blames the lover for her sister's death and goes to the hill town to confront him. There she learns that her sister was murdered. She also falls in love with the same man, who has disguised himself. The murder mystery falls by the wayside as both lovers dally on the lush hill slopes but, just when you've got your tap shoes on, a pair of likely suspects emerge, apparently bent on further foul play. In the end, the murder is wrapped up neatly while the two lovers cavort.

Comment: Long before the Internet search engine of the same name, India had her own Yahoo. Shammi Kapoor's remarkable dancing style—

part-Elvis, part-jitterbugger, wholly original—which marked him apart from all the other twist-and-shout musical heroes of the rock 'n' roll 1950s and earned him the well-deserved nickname, Yahoo. Asha Parekh was one of his most familiar screen cohorts. By 1966, both had grown a little too long in the tooth, and heavy in the hips, for such yahooistic wildness, but producer Nasir Hussain, who created his own highly successful and entertaining brand of musical romance over the next four decades, packaged the right vehicle for them to dance out the door. He started right off the bat by hiring Vijay 'Goldie' Anand whose deft ability to direct suspense drama and musical romance equally well helped turn *Teesri Manzil* into a wonderful mélange. Producer Hussain also introduced a production device that has since become a staple of film production, especially by today's mammoth music companies-turned-producers—he recycled script elements, the star pair, and even the locations from his previous smash hit *Dil Deke Dekho* (1959) which was a reworking of *Tumsa Nahin Dekha* (1957) which in turn was…well, you get the point. It was ironic that 25 years or so later, *Teesri Manzil* would be ripped off (and mixed with the plot of the Hollywood film *A Kiss Before Dying*) in the 1993 smash hit *Baazigar*. *Teesri Manzil* was a surprisingly fun rehash of the old swinging-boy-meets-straight-girl formula, livened by Shammi Kapoor's energetic antics, RD Burman's music (Panchimda, as he was affectionately known, grew decisively out of his legendary father SD Burman's shadow with this and other musical hits of the same decade), and singers Mohammed Rafi and Asha Bhosle's classic renditions of the film's still-hummable duets. As for the location recycling, millennial Hindi film audiences are inured to seeing the house in which the hero lives in one film used as the setting for the climax of a second, a song situation in a third, and a Governor's bungalow in a fourth! But back then, it was a novelty and like any novelty, fun in itself. In fact, that's what movies like *Teesri Manzil* were in those drainpipe-trouser, miniskirted years—pure fun.

Highlights: Shammi Kapoor's madcap song delivery style, especially in numbers like 'Deewana mujhsa nahin' and 'O haseena zulfonwali.' The mandatory Helen cabaret—a mainstay of Hindi films for over a decade—becomes a classic Bollywood highlight with 'Aaja aaja,' sexily rendered by Asha Bhosle. Bhosle's rendition of 'O mere sona re sona re,' which was recently the lead track of her best-selling tribute album to music director RD Burman (who was also allegedly her real-life lover) titled *Rahul And Me*.

More Like This: Dil Deke Dekho, Tumsa Nahin Dekha, any Shammi Kapoor starrer prior to 1970.
Kiss-Kitsch Rating: 4/5

Jewel Thief (1967)

Producer: Navketan Films. Director: Vijay Anand.

Cast: Dev Anand, Ashok Kumar, Vyjayanthimala, Tanuja, Helen, Fariyal, Anju Mahendru, Nasir Hussain, Sapru, Pratima Devi.

Ishtory: The old movie staple of identical lookalikes got a clever new twist in this cult thriller. The son of a police commissioner keeps getting mistaken for a notorious jewel thief. When a woman claims he had promised to marry her—and her brother seconds her claim, he decides enough is enough. He assumes the identity of the gem grabber and infiltrates his gang, romancing his woman as well. Meanwhile, the thief seems to have taken over the cop's identity! Shades of *Face/Off?* Not quite. The twist is that there is no jewel thief lookalike at all. He's just a fictional creation intended to confuse and trap the bad guys. He is authenticated by his sister, but he eventually turns out not to be her brother at all!

Comment: This is the cult Bollywood hit that established the brothers Anand as the bosses of slick musical crime thrillers. Vijay Anand topped earlier Navketan directors like Raj Khosla and Guru Dutt by bringing in the Western tech trappings—push-button doors, hidden bars, secret rooms, concealed safes, aeroplane stunts, ski slopes, snowlifts, foreign locations—that would become the staple of Bollywood crime thrillers for the next thirty years. The colour photography has that classic kitsch look of the period. The hit songs gave the film a repeat value that kept audiences coming back even after the vital suspense twist was revealed.

Highlights: The James Bond push-button gadgets sprinkled throughout. SD Burman's superhit-score. Kishore Kumar's rendition of 'Yeh dil na hota bechara,' Lata Mangeshkar's rendition of 'Rulake gaya sapna mera' and 'Hoton pe aisi baat main dubake chali aayi.' Ashok Kumar's deliberate misuse of his trustworthy image to create the plot-twist shocker.

More Like This: Johnny Mera Naam, Shaan, Azad, Jugnu, Don.
Kiss-Kitsch Rating: 3/5

Upkaar (1967)

Producer/Director: Manoj Kumar (Vishal Pictures).

Cast: Asha Parekh, Manoj Kumar, Pran, Kamini Kaushal, Prem Chopra, Kanhaiyalal, Madan Puri, Manmohan Krishna, David.

Ishtory: Bharat, a simple son-of-the-soil farmer whose name means India in Hindi, slaves on the family fields to pay for his younger brother's college education in the big bad city. City brother, corrupted by the decadent lifestyle of urban dwellers, squanders all the hard-earned savings and comes under the influence of the same anti-national criminal who had murdered their father. The criminal encourages a rift between the brothers over ownership of the family property—a genuine real-life cause of such rifts today. Disheartened by his brother's betrayal, Bharat quits the farm to join the Indian Army where he becomes a war hero, survives a murder attempt and befriends a crippled veteran. Meanwhile, bad younger brother sees the error of his ways and uses his knowledge of a nationwide smuggling and black-marketing network to help the police crack the whole gang, striking his own patriotic blow against the forces destroying India. In an unusual gesture of modernism, the heroine (top-billed star Asha Parekh) saves Bharat's life by operating on him at the climax.

Comment: Rejoice, fellow countrymen. With this film, Bharat was born. Not Bharat desh, the Hindi name of our proud nation India. We're talking about Bharat the speechifying do-gooding nationalistic hero portrayed by Manoj Kumar through a series of patriotic films over the last four decades of the 20th century. Manoj Kumar, an unlikely sensitive-featured weepy-eyed film hero, invented the Bharat persona in the wake of the India-Pakistan war of 1965. After giving Bharat the respectability of the old rapidly-vanishing India through his farming roots, and the masculine pride of a war veteran, he further delighted the impoverished Hindi film audiences by ranting against the nouveau riche urban jetsetters with their lavish possessions and luxurious lifestyles. Through the corruption and subsequent recanting of the younger brother's character, he confirmed the widespread suspicion of most have-not viewers that all luxuries and modern comforts were the ill-gotten products of illicit income gained through black-marketing, smuggling or other wheeling-dealing. The film's nationalism was genuine and heartfelt—it would be a few decades before Bharat began to seem like a caricature of his patriotic persona—and struck a powerful chord in the Pakistan-fearing-and-hating film audience. The film marked the reinvention of several people in new avatars: Manoj Kumar's highly successful new persona and his establishment as a commercially viable producer/director; Asha Parekh's changeover from a wild, hip-shaking romantic heroine to more dignified romantic heroine roles; former screen villain Pran's make-over as a sympathetic character actor, launching a new, extremely successful second career for himself; and Prem Chopra's subsequent typecasting as a highly successful villain following *Upkaar*. Manoj Kumar later attempted to follow through on his successful reinvention by campaigning for the Bharatiya Janata Party in 1991 but allegedly a problem with alcoholism prevented him actively entering politics. In a later interview, he described *Upkaar* as a "16,000-foot-long celluloid flag of India."

Highlights: Manoj Kumar's bhaashan-baazi (speeches and rhetoric), paving the way for heroes whose words speak louder than their actions. The blatant promotion of Government propaganda, especially the Congress Party's Jai jawan jai kisan (Hail soldier, hail farmer) campaign. Kalyanji-Anandji's string of hit songs, including 'Mere desh ki dharti,' 'Har khushi ho wahan' and 'Kasme vaade,' penned by lyricists Prem Dhawan, Indivar, Gulshan Bawra and Qamar Jalalabadi.

More Like This: Purab Aur Paschim, Hindustan Ki Kasam, Saat Hindustani, Kranti, Deshwasi, Border.

Kiss-Kitsch Rating: 2/5

Padosan (1968)

Producer: Mehmood (Mehmood Productions). Director: Jyoti Swaroop.

Cast: Sunil Dutt, Saira Banu, Kishore Kumar, Mehmood, Om Prakash, Mukri, Agha, Keshto Mukherjee.

Ishtory: An adaptation of the Bengali cult hit *Pasher Babu* written by Arun Choudhury. An innocent brahmachari (celibate Brahmin, shaven head with single-strand ponytail, caste marks and all) falls head over heels for his sultry neighbour. He's too simple-minded to see how hopelessly outclassed he is, or that every other man in sight is after the same girl—including her classical music tutor and his uncle! He soon learns that music is the way to her heart. And that she's most accessible when training at her window, which is opposite his window. The only problem is, he can't sing to save his life. So he discovers what every Hindi film hero has been doing since the start of Hindi sound cinema—playback singing! With his music tutor singing from behind the furniture, the simpleton sings his way into the girl's heart.

Comment: Film comedian Mehmood decided to produce this film as a vehicle for his own talents. That's why he gave himself the most potentially scene-stealing role—apart from the hero's, of course. He packed the rest of the cast with known comedic actors, all friends. The only gamble he took was by casting a relatively unknown young actor, Kishore Kumar. As things turned out, that young gadfly stole the show right from under the nose of Mehmood's and the rest of the cast. The younger brother of film star Ashok Kumar, Kishore Kumar, insisted on singing his own songs in the film, and on 'meddling' with the compositions and renditions as well. The director and other actors and playback singers were alarmed at the madcap on-set shenanigans of this young upstart. But Mehmood, sensing a talent emerging, convinced them all to allow Kishore Kumar free reign. The result was the most hilarious uninhibited comedy Hindi film had ever experienced. It took several hours of convincing before renowned Carnatic vocalist Manna Dey would let the brash unknown Kishore Kumar upstage him in the now-famous jugalbandi (duet) sequence. Kishore Kumar's antics on set became as legendary as his on-screen performance. His wild, exhilarated performance was unlike anything Hindi film crew—and film audiences—had seen before, with ad lib phrases and sounds inserted in mid-dialogue and mid-song without warning, chewing betelnut paan incessantly, waggling his eyebrows, thrashing on the floor in a paroxysm of musical ecstasy. Not only was the film a smash hit but it quickly became regarded as a cult comic classic, a status it still holds. But amazingly, so successful was Kishore Kumar's performance that every producer, director and star in town shied away from hiring or working with him. They feared he would upstage them the way he did everyone else in *Padosan*! Never again did any producer give him as much license as his friend and fellow comic Mehmood, and eventually Kishore Kumar would have to produce his own star vehicles to provide a platform for his unique acting style.

Highlights: Kishore Kumar's use of jazz-scat technique in his renditions. The jugalbandi 'Ek chatur naar.' The window song 'Mere saamne waali khidki mein.'

More Like This: Chalti Ka Naam Gaadi, Bombay To Goa.

Kiss-Kitsch Rating: 5/5

Johnny Mera Naam (1970)

Producer: Trimurti Films. Director: Vijay Anand.

Cast: Dev Anand, Hema Malini, Premnath, Jeevan, IS Johar, Pran, Sajjan, Padma, Randhawa, Iftikhar, Sulochana.

Ishtory: That old chestnut—brothers separated at birth growing up to become a cop and a goon—gets the Navketan treatment. Mr Bad Guy kills the police officer who was trying to crimp his style and steals one of his two infant sons, raising the kid to be his chief henchman. Post-opening credits, the other brother, now following in daddy's cop steps, infiltrates the outfit with the help of a beautiful woman whose father is being held hostage by the same (busy, busy) gang. In the end, both brothers are reunited and team up to destroy Mr Bad Guy.

Comment: O Brother, Where Art Thou? Right here beside you, bhai! Director Vijay 'Goldie' Anand and star Dev Anand teamed up for their third outing after *Jewel Thief* and *Guide*, with mixed results. The opening song sequence 'Kahin to nigahe' promises the now-established Navketan style and slickness, but none of the other songs have the same class. The chop-chop editing, non-stop soundtrack (soon to become a ear-bending staple in Bollywood), predictable script and average production design almost cut this film out of this book altogether. But these, you soon realise, are the result of the brothers working for an outside producer—so it's not a Navketan film at all. Why would a hit director/star pair of brothers work for someone else? Because it paid well, silly. Once you're over the initial disappointment at not getting a Navketan film, there's plenty to enjoy, although it wouldn't hurt to keep your thumb poised over the scan button of your DVD remote. Some elements are genuine classics (see highlights below) and if the whole doesn't add up to the sum of its parts, well, that's true of almost every Hindi film.

Highlights: Kalyanji/Anandji's whistle-worthy music score. Kishore Kumar's 'Vaada to nibhaya' duet with sensuous-voiced Asha Bhosle—rapidly rising alongside big sis Lata Mangeshkar in the singer ranks. The first-ever quadruple role by comedian IS Johar, itself a spoof on filmi double roles. The glamorous depiction of smuggling—a staple of India's notorious alternate economy at the time. The concealing of drugs in Indian classical music instruments intended for export to the West—later copied by actual drug smugglers. The villain masquerading as a godman is a comment on the Western craze for Indian gurus. Kishore Kumar's rendition of 'Pal bhar ke liye koi hame pyar kar le.' Hema Malini's pigeon-among-the-cats role, so popular she would reprise it umpteen times through her career. Above all, the period nostalgia of the whole film—guys in drainpipe trousers and greased-back hair rushing around with guns in hand, the original stylewallah Dev Anand hamming it up to the hilt, and dreamgirl Hema's big-eyed chubby beauty.

More Like This: Jewel Thief, The Great Gambler, Shalimar, Dus Numbree.

Kiss-Kitsch Rating: 3/5

Mera Naam Joker (1970)

Alternative Title: *I Am A Clown*

Producer/Director: Raj Kapoor (RK Films).

Cast: Raj Kapoor, Manoj Kumar, Rishi Kapoor, Dharmendra, Dara Singh, Rajendra Kumar, Padmini, Ksiena Rabiankina, Simi Garewal, Achala Sachdev, Om Prakash, members of the Soviet State Circus and of the Gemini Circus.

Ishtory: If Raj Kapoor's famous Raju persona was an Indian avatar of Chaplin's Tramp then *Mera Naam Joker* was the Indian avatar of Chaplin's *Limelight*, taken to epic proportions. Raju, now an ageing paunchy circus clown, reminisces about his life and loves in three parts. The first is about the adolescent Raju, son of a trapeze artist, falling in love/lust with his high-school teacher and fantasising about becoming a famous clown. The second part is about Raju's early days at a Russian circus and his first love affair with a beautiful Russian performer. The climax comes when his mother collapses and the grief-stricken Raju has to continue performing. 'The show must go on' becomes the central theme of the third and final part. Raju befriends a young girl who disguises herself as a boy to avoid attracting unwanted male attention—a ploy obviously not successful since Raju discovers her secret and falls in love with her anyway. The film ends with Raju hosting a spectacular show, his last, with all his three fantasy women watching from the audience.

Comment: Raj Kapoor's desire to make bigger and bigger films finally peaked with this mammoth autobiographical epic. Six years in the making, four hours long in its final cut, and almost bankrupting the entire Kapoor family and RK Studios, this was his *Citizen Kane*, his *Gone With The Wind*, his *Ben-Hur*. This was the film by which he wished to be remembered forever. The clown persona, like the Raju vagabond persona he had used earlier, was clearly a metaphor for his life as a film star, with Bollywood the circus ring. Raj Kapoor mounted a sumptuous spectacle, importing the entire Russian State Circus and hiring a local circus for its animals. The use of the Russian circus was also his open tribute to the Russian people, to whom Raj Kapoor, *Awara* and his Raju persona were cult figures. The star cast was one of the largest ever assembled on a single studio floor. The memorable music score, still hummed and whistled even today, was a smash hit. A galaxy of lyricists penned beautiful lyrics—Shailendra, Hasrat Jaipuri, Neeraj, Prem Dhawan, Shailey Shailendra. And all his regular collaborators—scriptwriter KA Abbas, cinematographer Radhu Karmarkar—gave their best. But in the end the film collapsed like an elephant smothered by its own bulk. The clown's fantasy affairs with his three Devi-like women turn out to be infantile infatuations and juvenile lusts. His sentimental self-indulgence becomes a tiresome tirade of weepy moaning. It's a film that you feel you must see, yet when you're done watching it, you wish you hadn't. An essential factor for box-office success in Hindi films is the famous second half. You can get away with virtually any buffoonery in the first half, but after the interval you better deliver the goods. Which basically means, resolve your protagonist's problems and give the audience an emotionally satisfying ending. *Mera Naam Joker* does precisely the opposite, leaving the hero without a single real relationship in the end, and a lot of grieving over wasted opportunities and lost loves. Great for a ghazal (a 'somebody done somebody wrong' song) but not for a movie which promised so much more. The heavy-handed symbolism—the abandoned clown doll, the cracked mirror with the laughing face—didn't help lighten the load either. In the end, *Mera Naam Joker* remains a magnificent failure. A film with a great heart and a treasure trove of emotional richness, but nothing worthwhile to lavish that wealth on. Still, you might well come away feeling that the word 'magnificent' was more applicable than 'failure.' Judge for yourself.

Highlights: Rishi Kapoor's debut as a chubby private schoolboy lusting after his schoolteacher. Shankar-Jaikishen's unforgettable music, especially 'Jeena yahan, marna yahan' and 'Ay, bhai zara dekh ke chalo.' Shailendra's lyrics for these same two songs, both of which are now used as idioms in the Hindi language. The Russian circus gymnasts and trapeze artists. The mournful violin theme. The clown's epic monologue about the stages of life. The powerful adolescent eroticism in the portrayal of the three women, foreshadowing Raj Kapoor's obsession with sexy female protagonists in his later films.

More Like This: Yaadein (the Sunil Dutt one, not the Subhash Ghai one!)

Kiss-Kitsch Rating: 4/5

Angry Young Men
& Lovers On Motorcycles

It was official. The old Bollywood was dead and buried. A new, angry, bitter, harder-hitting Bollywood had arrived on the scene, riding an Enfield Bullet 350cc, a cigarette dangling from its lip, a gun at its side and a cop's badge in its wallet. Oh sure, there would be romance too. Maybe even a lot of it, to make up for its lack at other times. But Hindi movies had wised up, greased up and had come of age. No more Chaplinesque comics or do-gooding heroes. These bhidoos (dudes) were here to settle a score, a personal vendetta, and nothing would stop them. Not even the long arm of the law. Nobody embodied the bad new Bollywood more than a tall, gangly young man with a baritone voice and a chip on his shoulder the size of Maharashtra. His name was Bachchan, Amitabh Bachchan, and now that he had walked into the room things would never be the same again.

Zanjeer (1973)

Producer/Director: Prakash Mehra (Prakash Mehra Productions).

Cast: Amitabh Bachchan, Jaya Bhaduri, Ajit, Binu, Pran, Om Prakash, Iftikhar, Ram Mohan, Yunus Pervez, Purnima, Gulshan Bawra, Keshto Mukherjee.

Ishtory: A child witnesses the murder of his parents by a faceless killer. As a young man, Vijay remains obsessed with nightmares of the memory, and by visions of a white horse, the emblem on the killer's bracelet. Starting as a scrupulously honest and upright police officer (the archetypal Hindi film hero), he begins to crave justice beyond the bounds of the law and descends into a crime-fighting vigilante. Befriending a Pathan (a Muslim of Afghani descent living in the North West Frontier province of former India (now in Pakistan), who wears a turban but no beard, carries a hardwood cane, speaks in a very typical accent and dialect), he seeks out his parents' murderer and his henchmen and avenges their murder, finally catharsising himself of his emotional angst.

Comment: This is it. The film that changed Hindi film history and catapulted its cast and crew into the realm of superstardom overnight. Writers Salim Khan and Javed Akhtar are said to have combined their skills to form an unbeatable writing team in Bombay's script-starved film industry. The legend goes that Salim Khan was the idea-and-concept genius while Javed Akhtar was a brilliant dialogue writer, and both collaborated equally on the screenplay, which Salim Khan presented colourfully and forcefully (singing snatches of song, miming fist fights and gunshots, delivering entire monologues from the script). Even so, it took a failed lyricist to recognise their talent. Prakash Mehra, the director of the successful *Haseena Maan Jayegi*, had suffered four painful flops after his hit debut. When he was regaled by the full Salim/Javed treatment of this revenge melodrama, he decided to throw everything at it. Boldly casting the well-known but decidely unstarry young Amitabh Bachchan in the lead role, he set out to capture the sense of angst and seething frustration of an entire generation of young Indian men. These men were caught between the dubious glamour of legit and illicit bijness on one hand, and waning fields like agriculture and government/professional employment on the other hand. The script, the producer/director's ability to stick to it all through the making, and the historic performance of Amitabh Bachchan made this an instant film classic. Yet, *Zanjeer* is much less than the sum of its parts. Seen today, every element of this delicious khichdi (a preparation of boiled rice and lentils steamed together) has been topped in later films: Amitabh Bachchan went on to deliver a whole career full of far superior performances; Salim/Javed outshone themselves in any number of scripts; producer/director Prakash Mehra outdid *Zanjeer* at least half a dozen times; Kalyanji/Anandji composed far more memorable music and songs before and after *Zanjeer*. Yet *Zanjeer* is worth watching for the emergence of a persona that every Hindi film-goer later took for granted, because it traces every step of the development of Vijay, the persona that would capture the imagination of an entire nation. Amitabh Bachchan and his Vijay persona are inseparable in our minds today. It was in this film that he shed his inhibiting cliché roles and donned the garments of a character type that made him the greatest superstar in India, and lent a face and voice to a lonely frustration that was burning within every young man. Just as similar characters in American films like *Taxi Driver* and novels like *A Catcher In The Rye* captured American angst, *Zanjeer* brought to life our Vijay side. It took Amitabh Bachchan almost another 30 years and as many films to grow out of the shadow of the Vijay legend.

Highlights: Amitabh Bachchan's magnificently conflicted cop struggling to overcome his scruples and turn vigilante. Amitabh Bachchan's scenes with Jaya Bhaduri, soon to become Jaya Bachchan. Amitabh Bachchan's almost Jekyll & Hyde changeover to the vigilante Vijay, the reason why a string of stars such as Dev Anand and Raaj Kumar had turned down the role earlier. Salim/Javed's taut linear screenplay and masterful Urdu dialogue. Producer/director Prakash Mehra's simple but effective production and stylishly naturalistic narrative approach.

More Like This: Muqqadar ka Sikandar, Deewar, Trishul, Khoon Pasina, Hera Pheri, Kaalia, Agneepath, almost any other Amitabh Bachchan film between 1973 and 1993.

Kiss-Kitsch Rating: 4/5

Bobby (1973)

Producer/Director: Raj Kapoor (RK Films).

Cast: Rishi Kapoor, Dimple Kapadia, Pran, Premnath, Durga Khote.

Ishtory: The most famous Bollywood version of the classic Romeo & Juliet love saga, based on the novel by scriptwriter KA Abbas. A young rich boy, neglected by his parents, returns home from boarding school to celebrate his 18th birthday. He meets and falls in love with Bobby, the beautiful young Catholic daughter of his former nanny Mrs Braganza. Their young infatuation soon blossoms into a full-blown romance through a series of secret rendezvous. When their parents discover the romance, a storm erupts. Besides the classic rich/poor divide, a familiar Bollywood device, there's also the religious difference to contend with. Despite their highly sophisticated outlook, the boy's parents can't accept a meat-eating, booze-swirling Goan Catholic fisherman as their in-law. The young lovers elope, preferring to die rather than be separated. The film ends with the famous scene in which both fathers leap into a raging river to rescue each other's kids, bonding instantly and resolving their differences.

Comment: Bobby marks the first film in legendary thespian/auteur Raj Kapoor's famous third phase. After unsuccessfully attempting to extend his middle-aged career with the spectacular failure of *Mera Naam Joker*, he faced a serious financial crisis. *Bobby* was his lifeboat. Launching his young son Rishi Kapoor (earlier seen as the chubby young boy in *Mera Naam Joker*) as the romantic lead, he helmed this sugary sweet love story designed to please the young audiences who were tired of seeing paunchy older couples frolicking past their prime. He also stirred in a good dose of sexiness, playing on the chubby attractiveness of his fresh new heroine Dimple Kapadia, and deftly playing up the erotic undertones that had characterised all his films. *Bobby*'s success was not just due to its typical young-doomed-lovers reprise but to this clever exploitation of teenage sexuality. Another film released a year or so later, *Julie*, successfully mined the same formula—the heroine's Catholic background providing an excuse to show her in waist-high miniskirts at every opportunity. *Bobby* played on the Indian fascination for Christian/Western liberalism of dress, habit and attitude. The girl's father (the unforgettable Premnath) brought alive the boisterous fun-loving booze-swilling character of the Goan Catholics with remarkable accuracy, while creating an instant stereotype that would later be sorely misused by lesser film-makers. Bobby is portrayed as the ultimate jailbait tease. Her portrayal would have caused major controversy had she been a Hindu girl in the film, especially in those conservative 70s. In later films like *Ram Teri Ganga Mailee* and *Satyam Shivam Sundaram*, Raj Kapoor was so fascinated with young female flesh that the naked female form seemed to be more important than the story! But in *Bobby*, he managed to find the perfect blend of adolescent lust and the excitement of young/first love. The film brought in the much-needed moolah and a new genre was born.

Highlights: Dimple Kapadia in a bikini, or in a saree, or just in any scene. Rishi Kapoor's lovable zest. Shailendra Singh's debut as a singer, singing playback for Rishi Kapoor. Laxmikant/Pyarelal sensational hit score: 'Main shayar to nahin,' 'Mujhe kuch kehna hain,' 'Jhoot bole kawa kaate' and the classic 'Hum tum ek kamre mein bandh ho' with its apt use of the accordion (later used by Laxmikant/Pyarelal to great effect in their score for *Amar Akbar Anthony*). Singer Narendra Chanchal's rendition of the high-pitched tragic song 'Beshak mandir-masjid tod do.' Piloo Wadia's hilarious caricature of the Parsi woman. Aruna Irani's sultry older seductress. Prem Chopra's menacing villainy. Premnath's boisterous joie de vivre. Pran's suave control-freak father.

More Like This: Julie, Love Story, Quyamat Se Quyamat Tak, Maine Pyar Kiya.

Kiss-Kitsch Rating: 4/5

Sholay (1975)

Alternative Titles: *Embers, Flames Of The Sun*

Producer: GP Sippy (Sippy Films). Director: Ramesh Sippy.

Cast: Dharmendra, Sanjeev Kumar, Amitabh Bachchan, Hema Malini, Jaya Bhaduri, Amjad Khan, Iftikhar, AK Hangal, Leela Mishra, Macmohan, Sachin, Asrani, Helen, Keshto Mukherjee.

Ishtory: Backstory: The zamindar of a North Indian village is also a decorated cop posted at the nearest big town. When a gang of dacoits terrorises the region, he wages a personal war against them, finally capturing their leader and sending him to jail for a long time. The dacoit leader busts out and returns to wreak vengeance—he slaughters the cop's family, right down to the smallest kid. Only the cop's daughter-in-law sur-vives because she's out visiting her parents. The cop returns and chases after the dacoit, but is captured. Instead of killing him, the dacoit lopes off his arms with a sword, rendering him harmless. The film begins when the cop hires two small-time crooks to hunt down and kill the dacoit. The two ruffians grow attached to the villagers and the job becomes personal, with them willing to go to any lengths to wipe out the dacoit gang brutal-ising the villagers. Both also fall in love, one with a horse-rickshaw driver and the other with the zamindar's widowed daughter-in-law. But in the end, only one of them survives the final encounter with the gang, pay-ing the price for vengeance while fulfilling their task.

Comment: If you had to see just one Hindi film in your life, just one, then see *Sholay*. It's deservedly considered the most perfect Hindi film ever made. So much so that several critics insist that innovation in Hindi films ends with *Sholay* and that everything after that is repetitious trash. That's a harsh and unfair judgement. There's been much good work since *Sholay*, and much more yet to come, certainly. But you might understand the sentiment if you sit through a few hundred hours of other hit films and then spend a couple of hours watching *Sholay*. It's not perfect by a long stretch but it's like a breath of fresh air in a stale auditorium. Inspired heavily by Japanese samurai epics and American and Italian Westerns, most obviously The *Magnificent Seven* (which was based on Akira Kuro-sawa's *Seven Samurai*), *Sholay* is a magnificent spectacle which delivers everything you'd want in a movie: action, romance, comedy, tragedy, emotional depth, music, dance, even two cleverly placed cabarets! Every scene, every character, every shot, every line of dialogue, song lyric, composition is perfectly timed and delivered. *Sholay* is a film that uses all the cliché conventions yet somehow manages to reinvent them in a way that seems magical and wonderfully entertaining. Opening to a dismal reception, the film was written off as a flop in the first week. Apparently, the Sippys called an emergency meeting with writers Salim/Javed and rising star Amitabh Bachchan (third-billed in *Sholay* but already a super-star). The Sippys debated pulling the film out of theatres and reshooting and re-editing substantially. But Salim/Javed had such faith in their script that they asked them to wait a week longer. Their confidence was well placed. Word of mouth brought audiences thronging to the theatres in the second and third weeks. (Those were slower-paced, more forgiving years for Bollywood—today, a film that doesn't open big on the first weekend is likely to be pulled out within a week). In a month, it was a rage. In a year, it was still running to packed houses and was universally accepted as a modern classic. Five years later, it was still running and every viewer was repeating the dialogue and song lyrics by heart. Even today, *Sholay* still draws packed halls on re-release. What is the magic of this film? Well, the good news is it's all up there on the screen for you to see. From the antics of the ridiculously caricaturish comedic characters to the rakish charm of Dharmendra, the brooding pauses of Amitabh, the angry frustration of Sanjeev Kumar, the fatalistic silence of Jaya Bachchan, the wild-eyed evil of Gabbar Singh (played by Amjad Khan), you're likely to come out feeling that *Sholay* is a film packed with great, unforgettable characters. True. But it's also a film of great moments: Veeru and Jay (Amitabh and Dharamendra) on their bike singing about eternal friendship, Gabbar Singh forcing Basanti (Hema Malini) to dance on broken glass to keep her lover alive, Gabbar Singh's massacre of the Thakur's family with the sound effect of the rusty swing on the soundtrack, Veeru pretending to be the voice of God exhorting Basanti to marry him, Veeru threatening to commit 'soside' from the top of a water tower, Jai mucking up Veeru's marriage proposal, Asrani's Chaplinesque warden telling half his men to go right, half to go left and the rest to follow him, the blind man groping for the corpse of his dead son...*Sholay* is a hundred unforgettable moments that linger with you for years afterward. Even now, I can remember the first time I saw it, at Geeta Talkies in the Worli neighbourhood of midtown Bombay, in an almost-deserted auditorium, feeling like I'd found the mother lode of entertainment, and then going back to see it a dozen or more times over the years—always with a full house—and never tiring of it. If you want to see just one Hindi film, this is indeed the one.

Highlights: RD Burman's fabulous background score and songs: 'Yeh dosti,' 'Aa jab tak hain jaan' and his gruff rendition of 'Mehbooba re mehbooba.' Amjad Khan's portrayal of Gabbar Singh, a role with which he was identified till his early death almost twenty years later, especially his famous "Are o, Samba" and "Are o, Kaalia" dialogue. Dwarka Divecha's camerawork which transforms North-Central India into a setting straight out of a Sam Peckinpah Western. Salim/Javed's story, screenplay and dialogue surpassing even their masterpiece *Deewar*, released the same year as *Sholay*.

More Like This: Mera Gaon Mera Desh, Hum Paanch, Khote Sikke, Kachche Heere, Jaanbaaz.

Kiss-Kitsch Rating: 6/5 (5/5 just ain't good enough for this curry Western!)

Deewar (1975)

Producer: Gulshan Rai (Trimurti Films). Director: Yash Chopra.

Cast: Amitabh Bachchan, Shashi Kapoor, Nirupa Roy, Neetu Singh, Parveen Babi, Manmohan Krishna, Madan Puri, Iftikhar, Sudhir, Rajpal, Jagdish Raj, Kuljit Singh, Rajkishore, AK Hangal.

Ishtory: Vijay and Ravi, two brothers, react differently to their childhood humiliation and struggle after their father is wrongfully accused of being a thief—Ravi becomes a cop, Vijay a criminal. Inevitably, their paths cross and the cop makes the arrest of his brother a personal goal. Their mother, the epitome of Hindu dharmic virtue, becomes their mutual bone of contention, finally choosing the side of righteousness by turning her back on the criminal son. The long arm of the law eventually triumphs, and Vijay dies after making a spectacular appearance at the temple where he was to meet his mother one last time, delivering the mandatory deathbed speech. Salim/Javed's brilliant script was said to be partly inspired by the real-life career of notorious smuggler Haji Mastan.

Comment: Deewar was totally unlike *Sholay*, despite being scripted by the same writers. While *Sholay* proved to be impossible to top or imitate, *Deewar* continued the Vijay persona that Bachchan had first embodied in his breakthrough hit *Zanjeer*. After *Deewar*'s phenomenal success, Bachchan *was* Vijay, and vice versa. The film was released at a particularly delicate point in Indian history. Prime Minister Indira Gandhi had been under attack in the Supreme Court by opposing political forces, and she responded by declaring a national state of Emergency. It was a time comparable to the McCarthy hearings in 1950s USA and film-makers were careful not to tread on the censor board's sensitive toes. So, even though the character of Vijay in *Deewar* was clearly inspired by real-life smuggling tycoon Haji Mastan, great care was taken to punish the bad guy and denounce him repeatedly, while cleverly using the hedonistic criminal lifestyle to add glamour to the film. A familiar device, but in *Deewar* it was used brilliantly to mirror the frustration of the country's working class as well. Vijay is essentially a good man, the hero of the film despite his wrongdoings, and his descent into the criminal underworld is clearly blamed on circumstances and external pressures. He is, in effect, the middle-class educated Indian of the mid-70s, struggling to get a job in a corrupt system, to make ends meet through honest labour, while all around him smugglers, black marketeers and openly dishonest profiteers enjoy the ill-gotten fruits of their immoral efforts. Growing up in Bombay in that period, meeting both the black-market folk and the white-market folk, I can testify that Vijay's frustration and despair were real and genuine. The fact that Haji Mastan emerged from his jail term to become a reformed, highly respected member of society despite his past misdoings, was concrete proof that the system had broken down from within. But *Deewar* was also a terrifically entertaining crime thriller, the action sequences clearly inspired by Hong Kong action flicks, and Amitabh's lanky surliness and mother obsession are the stuff of legend. See this for him alone, or for the film as a reflection of India in those dark and hopeless 70s, but see it you must.

Highlights: The scene under the bridge between Amitabh Bachchan and Shashi Kapoor with the famous dialogue: "Mere paas Ma hain." Amitabh's dying scene in the temple at the climax where he rails and rants against God before dying in his mother's arms—much-imitated, especially by Shah Rukh Khan in *Baazigar*. The device of Vijay's lucky billa no. 786, considered a lucky number by Muslims in India. (A billa is a numeral identification tag, like the ones sown onto the uniforms of Indian railway porters or dock workers. Although now they're all cloth, they used to be metal.) Salim/Javed's brilliant script, using one long extended flashback to tell the entire story. Nirupa Roy's iconic portrayal of the mother, regarded by critics as a symbol of India, the 'mother nation,' an integral part of Bollywood iconography. Nobody played Mama better! And above all, Amitabh Bachchan—even today, more than a quarter century later, after watching his most recent releases *Ek Rishta* and *Aks*, you realise that you were right all along: There's never been an actor like him anywhere in the world. Magnificent is too small a word.

More Like This: Muqaddar Ka Sikandar, Khoon Pasina, Don, Kaalia, Trishul.

Kiss-Kitsch Rating: 4/5

Keep The Faith

Film audiences had endorsed the new, angrier Bollywood but all punch and no rum-punch makes Jaikishen a dull boy, right? So they spiked the buttermilk, mixing a little goofball entertainment with the vendetta melodramas. Even some religious fantasy that crossed the border into everyday reality. Movies were movies after all. Give them drama. Give them social issues. Heck, give them Gods and monsters too. But above all, give them entertainment.

Jai Santoshi Maa (1975)

Producer: Bhagyalakshmi Chitra Mandir. Director: Vijay Sharma.

Cast: Anita Guha, Ashish Kumar, Kanan Kaushal, Trilok Kapoor, Mahipal, Manhar Desai, BM Vyas, Bharat Bhushan.

Ishtory: A devout disciple of a lesser-known Goddess earns the envy of the wives of the Holy Trinity of Hindu Gods, Brahma, Vishnu and Shiva. To test her devotion, they create a number of obstacles in her path. When she succeeds despite these divine hindrances, her deity wreaks her anger on the three Goddesses. Impressed by her mortal devotee's faith, they accept her into the pantheon of major Gods, while on earth her loyal worshipper finds happiness and success as a reward for her trials.

Comment: The mythological film has always been a staple of Hindi cinema, but in the 1950s increasing urbanisation made film-makers switch to more socially relevant stories. By the 1970s mythological movies were seen as downmarket and vernac, suitable only for films made in other ethnic Indian languages. (Vernac is short for vernacular. It is a common Indian English word for a person of an ethnic Indian background without much education, English or sophistication who speaks only a local 'vernacular' language. The equivalent of a country bumpkin or backwoods bozo.) So when this low-budget B-movie broke all records to become one of the highest-grossing films of the year—and this was the same year in which blockbuster hits like *Deewar* and *Sholay* were released—it took everyone by surprise. The film was cheaply made and it showed: the special effects were crude, the actors complete unknowns, and even the Devi (Goddess) portrayed was virtually unheard of! But something about the film enraptured audiences. It had a sense of faith that was missing from most other films of the time. While Amitabh Bachchan was shooting up dacoits or flinging bad guys out high-storey windows in cynical Western-influenced blockbusters, this little film crept in through the back door and whispered, "Remember who you are, remember to believe." The theme of devotion despite all odds is a great Indian philosophy. It underlies the Hindu sense of implicit trust in fate, which is often mistaken for fatalism. Satyavati's unswerving devotion to her Goddess defies even the Gods, proving that faith can work miracles. It was a message that Indian audiences, weary of the disappointments of the post-Independence years, distrustful of politicians and administrators, living from hand-to-mouth to survive, struggling with the high levels of educated unemployed, hatefully jealous of the widespread corruption and organised crime visible in the cities, needed to believe. They thronged to theatres in fantastic numbers, leaving their footwear outside cinema halls, briefly turning the theatre into a temple, and chanted and prayed along with the long-suffering protagonist, cheering wet-eyed when she was finally vindicated and blessed by the Devi. This wasn't a film, it was a phenomenon. See it in that light and you might come to believe too.

Highlights: C Arjun's hugely popular music, especially the hit aarti song (prayer chant) 'Main to aarti utaaru re, Santoshi Mata ki.'

More Like This: You tell me!

Kiss-Kitsch Rating: 2/5

Amar Akbar Anthony (1977)

Producer/Director: Manmohan Desai.

Cast: Vinod Khanna, Rishi Kapoor, Amitabh Bachchan, Neetu Singh, Shabana Azmi, Parveen Babi, Nirupa Roy, Jeevan, Pran, Helen.

Ishtory: Three brothers are separated at birth from each other and from their mother by a dastardly villain. The three boys are raised by foster parents of three different faiths: Hindu (Amar), Muslim (Akbar) and Christian (Anthony). The villain tries to pit the three brothers against each other but they discover their blood relationship and unite against their common foe, eventually destroying the villain and rescuing their mother while finding time to romance three beautiful damsels en route. Colour.

Comment: Amar Akbar Anthony marked the pinnacle of Bollywood kitsch. In this landmark entertainer, the genre literally seemed to mock its own devices! Director Manmohan Desai took all the disparate elements of Hindi commercial cinema—separated at birth, vendetta, brothers pitted against each other, the long-suffering mother—and raised them to iconic status. Like other 70s angry young man epics, *Amar Akbar Anthony* bore similarities to the later heroic bloodshed films of Hong

Kong. Even the slow-mo fight sequences and intense close-ups of sweat flying and fists punching flesh are all there. Amitabh Bachchan's scenes with his Ma (Nirupa Roy now firmly established as the Mother India of Bollywood) carry echoes of his other, more intense, bad beta (son) roles in films like *Deewar*. But Desai's gloriously wild and wacky narrative style turned every scene, song and fight sequence into a highlight. In fact, the entire film is a series of highlights which somehow manages to add up to a full story. Despite the film's multi-star cast, it's evident that every actor, including Azmi who was an art cinema crossover, had a ball making this film. It's this sense of fun that makes it so enjoyable to watch even today. That, and the pleasure of watching a third-billed actor named Amitabh create one of the most endearing and enduring comic-hero roles in Hindi film history, makes *Amar Akbar Anthony* an essential part of any must-see list of Hindi films.

Highlights: Amitabh Bachchan leaping out of a giant Easter Egg in a top hat and tails, singing 'My name is Anthony Gonsalves.' Amitabh Bachchan drunk and arguing with his reflection in a mirror. Amitabh Bachchan disguised as a Catholic priest apologising to Jesus for resorting to violence. Amitabh Bachchan spouting the tapori basha (street slang) that later became the dialogue norm for Bollywood action heroes. Jeevan's sneering villainy. The mother miraculously regaining her eyesight. The title song 'Honee ko anhonee kar do' and the campy qawali 'Parda hai parda.' (Qawali is a kind of Urdu song rendered by a lead singer with several backing singers. It is always sung kneeling down (on a mat of course!) and with great gusto, traditionally making up extempore lyrics with great wit and elegance of phrase. The singer is called a Qawal, the style qawali, the song a qawali.)

More Like This: Naseeb, Shaan, Tridev, Trimurti.

Kiss-Kitsch Rating: 4/5

Trishul (1978)

Producer/Director: Yash Chopra (Trimurti Films).

Cast: Amitabh Bachchan, Sanjeev Kumar, Raakhee, Shashi Kapoor, Prem Chopra, Hema Malini, Sachin, Poonam, Manmohan Krishna, Waheeda Rehman.

Ishtory: Legendary scriptwriting duo Salim/Javed seems to have combined the estranged father/son conflict of *Awara* and the characterisation of *Deewar* to pen this brilliantly developed screenplay. Bachchan, once again plays the archetypal angry young man character Vijay, suspects his father of having abandoned his mother. His obsession leads him down the familiar filmi path of crime and punishment, culminating in a series of action set pieces where his angst is released through brutal fist fights, ending in a climactic warehouse sequence.

Comment: There are no sequels in Hindi films. Well, there have been a couple of exceptions—*Khotte Sikke* and *Kacche Heere* are the only examples that spring readily to mind—but by and large, the concept of the serial film (*Indiana Jones, Star Wars, Die Hard, Lethal Weapon*) doesn't exist in India. In its place is a nebulous entity that we could call the persona or image film. So, for instance, we have Salman Khan, now hugely popular for his comedic-romantic persona, reprising the same bare-shirted loverboy in any number of films, usually all directed by David Dhawan. Or there's our action hero Sunny Deol, who's the closest to a poor Indian's Arnold we have. But the granddaddy of all the image personas in filmdom is undoubtedly Amitabh Bachchan's Vijay. Bachchan was a fine leading man for over a decade, but after the watershed *Zanjeer* (1973) his life and career and Hindi film history were changed forever. Bachchan's unconventional features and gangly, brooding presence had found their perfect screen expression. *Trishul* was one of several excellent films that simply took the persona into areas that had yet to be explored. Producer/director Yash Chopra, now acknowledged for his concern with character insights and relationships rather than the formulaic shoot-em-up exploitation of most 70s/80s flicks, cast *Trishul* with the same actors of his earlier smash critical and commercial hit *Deewar*, leaving out only the mother of Vijay, Nirupa Roy. The result was an electrifying face-off between two brilliant actors with sharply contrasting personalities and acting styles—Sanjeev Kumar as the father and Amitabh Bachchan as the son. Even when the film descends into the obligatory action sequences typical of the period, Bachchan's scenes are a treat to watch. In its play-off between the screen personas of two major stars, *Trishul* is similar to Hollywood casting coups such as the De Niro/ Pacino starrer *Heat*, or the later Bollywood hit *Saudagar* (1991). It also marks an important variation on the Oedipal theme of previous father/son films. Instead of attacking his father, as Raj Kapoor's Raju tried to do in *Awara*, Vijay sets out to destroy his business empire, playing on the growing Indian fascination for wealth acquired through non-agricultural methods.

Highlights: Salim/Javed's superb screenplay and dialogue, especially when writing for Vijay. The scenes featuring both Amitabh Bachchan and Sanjeev Kumar. Amitabh's look and personality, from his buffed hair right down to the flaring bell-bottoms and two-toned Italian-style shoes, came to represent the epitome of looking cool for a generation of Indian men who identified with Vijay's frustrations and angst.

More Like This: Awara, Mughal-e-Azam (for the father/son conflict), *Mashaal, Parampara, Mohabbatein.*

Kiss-Kitsch Rating: 4/5

Anything Goes

Bollywood audiences had seen it all, loved it all and wanted it all. The Hindi film didn't have one definite face any more. You could be personal, raw and autobiographical like a brilliant young film-maker who cut a vein and wrote on celluloid. You could put your political agenda into a streetwise film. You could promote your son as a star and expect viewers to pay for the privilege of launching his career. You could make fun of your city officials and your film institute colleagues. You could even deal with a frustrating terrorist problem the easy way—on film. That is, as long as you did it with a good-looking hero and heroine, plenty of good music, songs and dances, and delivered two and half hours of solid entertainment. The new Bollywood, available in every flavour you like and even some you don't.

Arth (1982)

Producer: Kuljit Pal (Anu Arts). Director: Mahesh Bhatt.

Cast: Shabana Azmi, Smita Patil, Kulbhushan Kharbanda, Raj Kiran.

Ishtory: An ad film-maker is torn between his devoted wife and a sultry model with whom he's having an affair. When his wife learns about the affair, she's shattered and leaves him. Her struggle to survive as a single working woman in conservative Indian society forms the bulk of the rest of the film. A friend professes his love for her but she resists the temptation to fall into another relationship. Meanwhile, her husband's mistress is torn by guilt over destroying his marriage and sinks into paranoid psychosis. When she grows violent, he leaves her and attempts to reconcile with his wife. She asks him a single question: "If I was the one who had been unfaithful and was asking you to take me back, would you accept?" His famous answer is a simple, honest "No." Her response is as shocking and triumphant. She shuts the door in his face and he walks away alone.

Comment: Mahesh Bhatt's first film *Manzilen Aur Bhi Hain* was banned for its over-the-top sex and violence. With *Arth*, he found his first major release and success. Coming to Bollywood out of left field, Bhatt brought an intellectual South-Bombay sensibility to Hindi films that was neither quite art film-like nor wholly commercial. Later, pressed by the need to make a living, he shed this inner vision for a more commercial approach. But in *Arth*, the sheer rawness of emotional revelation, the naked insight into man/woman relationships, the honest depiction of extramarital affairs, the destructive force of illicit sex and the resulting guilt leap out from every frame. The film is textured with an emotional brashness that's almost uncomfortable to watch. Bhatt later admitted in a personal interview that *Arth* was based on his affair with actress Parveen Babi and the subsequent breakdown of his marriage. His casting of Smita Patil was inspired. Her dusky, unconventional looks made her brilliant acting almost hypnotic to watch. Her portrayal of the increasingly paranoid psychotic model plagued with typical Indian guilt over wrecking another woman's marriage, is brutally honest and true to life. (Patil's brilliant career was cut short by her untimely death giving birth a few years later.) Shabana Azmi's weepy yet inwardly resilient wife is a perfectly realised character that has been imitated countless times since, inspiring a host of similar protagonists in films and even television serials like Neena Gupta's *Saans*. Kulbushan Kharbanda has never had a role that matches his abilities so well. Mahesh Bhatt's use of ghazals as background songs during the film—rather than the typical song-and-dance set pieces—was also inspired and apt. Today, despite its absence of a real 'story,' *Arth* retains the power to move and involve you in the emotional turmoil of its characters, in the same way that independent American films like *Leaving Las Vegas* do.

Highlights: Real-life husband/wife duo Jagjit Singh and Chitra Singh's haunting ghazals, composed and sung by themselves—'Aankhon mein nami hanseen labon pe.' Urdu poet Kaifi Azmi's lyrics. Stage and art film actress Rohini Hattangadi's letter-perfect portrayal of a Maharashtrian cleaning woman or bai. Real-life husband/wife pair Siddharth and Gita Kak's brief cameo as themselves. Raj Kiran's hangdog portrayal of the unrequited lover. Pravin Bhatt's shadowy camerawork, perfectly capturing the intense emotional turmoil of the characters. The performances of Smita Patil, Kulbushan Kharbanda and Shabana Azmi (who received her second Best Actress National Award for the role).

More Like This: Kaash.

Kiss-Kitsch Rating: 4/5

Betaab (1983)

Producer: Dharmendra (Vijayta Films). Director: Rahul Rawail.

Cast: Sunny Deol, Amrita Singh, Shammi Kapoor, Nirupa Roy, Prem Chopra.

Ishtory: An interesting slant on Shakespeare's *The Taming Of The Shrew*, a staple source of Hindi film scenarists. Iconic film writer-turned-lyricist Javed Akhtar conceived this action/romance set on a stud farm where everybody trembles under the tyranny of a petulant princess. She meets her match when her father hires a tough young farmhand and horse-breaker who won't tolerate her tantrums. The 'taming' of the 'shrew' inevitably leads to a passionate love affair. Papa and a villainous rival obstruct the lovers but the hero's hard-hitting fists and even harder-hitting passion win the day.

Comment: Just the year before, another former Hindi film star Rajendra Kumar had launched his teenage son Kumar Gaurav in the smash hit *Love Story.* So superstar Dharmendra decided the time was right to launch his scion, Ajay Singh Deol aka 'Sunny' Deol. Who better to helm the debut vehicle than the ghost director of *Love Story*, Rahul Rawail, son of the illustrious film-maker HS Rawail, and an directorial assistant to the great Raj Kapoor for seven years. To play the heroine, papa Dharmendra found the fresh-faced young daughter of a politician whose family name would also help the film's publicity. While Sunny Deol proved to be no Marlon Brando, he certainly brought a robust Punjabi earthiness that was refreshing amongst the crowd of chocolate-face heroes popular at the time. His inability to dance was more than offset by his mukka-baazi or prowess as a fighter. Director Rawail and Sunny created a persona of muscle and machismo, intensity and righteous rage, honesty and uprightness that launched Sunny as a star and remains his unique selling point. The critics were slower to applaud. It took another decade or so and a National Award for Best Actor in *Ghayal* to convince them that this Punjabi scrapper could act. But audiences, especially the profitable Northern and Punjab circuit so crucial to film distributors, loved him from the first. As his die-hard fans say even today, "Nobody can throw a punch as convincingly as Sunny Deol."

Highlights: Sunny's famous entry scene on a horse. Amrita Singh's feisty resistance. The refreshing stud farm and hilly locations—rare in an industry where most films are shot on sound stages and Bombay streets. Director Rawail's taut screenplay from Javed Akhtar's story idea.

More Like This: Sholay, Khote Sikke, Kachche Heere, Jaanbaaz.

Kiss-Kitsch Rating: 3/5

Jaane Bhi Do Yaaron (1983)

Producer: National Film Development Corporation (NFDC). Director: Kundan Shah.

Cast: Naseeruddin Shah, Ravi Baswani, Bhakti Bharve, Om Puri, Satish Shah, Pankaj Kapoor, Satish Kaushik, Neena Gupta, Deepak Qazir, Rajesh Puri, Zafar Sanjari, Vihu Vinod Chopra.

Ishtory: Two goofy press photographers are hired by the editor of a gossip magazine. Their assignment is to spy on a rich builder and the police commissioner of Bombay with a view to getting evidence of crooked dealings. They unearth the crooked dealings, but the police commissioner gets murdered when the deal goes sour. The only way they can prove the whole story is to get hold of the commissioner's corpse. A bizarre chase ensues in which everyone chases everyone, in the tradition of Hollywood mad-chase epics like *It's A Mad Mad Mad Mad World*. In the end, the photographers are blamed for the collapse of the flyover that was built by the crooked builder!

Comment: A sleeper hit that became a cult classic, it is still recalled fondly by Bollywood professionals and fans. The film used a goofball style of comedy that hadn't been seen since the heyday of actor/singer/director Kishore Kumar. The script is laced with references, both direct and satirical, to real Bombay personalities, including politicians and criminals! Produced on a shoestring budget, it was one of the few comedies made in the alternate cinema movement that had seen its peak in the 70s.

Highlights: The passing-the-parcel movements of the corpse. The collapse of the flyover shown using real footage of the Byculla Bridge flyover collapsing.

More Like This: Aankhen, Hera Pheri (2000), TV serials such as *Yeh Jo Hai Zindagi* and *Nukkad.*

Kiss-Kitsch Rating: 3/5

Ankush (1985)

Producer: Shilpa Movies. Director: N Chandra.

Cast: Madan Jain, Nana Patekar, Arjun Chakraborty, Suhas Palshikar, Nisha Singh, Ashalata, Dinkar Kaushik, Mahavir Shah, Rabia Amin, Ravi Patwardhan, Mastery Bobby, Raja Bundela, Sayyed.

Ishtory: A good gang of four educated unemployed young men virtually rule their inner-city mohalla (neighbourhood), getting involved in street fights, meting out street justice for petty crimes and waging an endless feud with a far more powerful bad gang. They are befriended and reformed by a neighbourhood beauty who pushes them to make something better of their lives. When she is gang-raped by the bad gang, the good gang reverts to their old street-fighting ways.

Comment: Ankush has been repeatedly labelled a Shiv Sena movie. It's worth taking a moment to understand the label. The Shiv Sena is a local Maharashtrian political group that mobilises young Hindu men to assert their right to employment and better living. The good gang depicted in the film is an accurate reflection of countless such small groups seen hanging on the streets of most Bombay neighbourhoods. Writer/director N Chandra claimed to have based the film on his youthful experiences, and both he and his main star Nana Patekar openly avowed loyalty to the Shiv Sena party. The film was a surprise hit, countering North Indian-dominated Bollywood with a rare Maharashtrian/Bombay subject. Made on a low budget using relatively unknown (and even inexperienced) actors, *Ankush* had an immediacy and rawness that was compelling and believable. Nana Patekar shot to fame as a major superstar, taking his *Ankush* persona (which seemed to reflect his real-life views) into a series of bombastic political vehicles. N Chandra found greater commercial success with *Tezaab* and inevitably drifted away from his inner-city roots to churn out a string of mediocre commercial potboilers. It would be another 15 years before films like *Satya* and *Vaastav* were able to effectively capture the reality of Bombay street life again.

Highlights: The streetwise performances of the young men, especially Nana Patekar.

More Like This: Arjun, Satya, Vaastav.

Kiss-Kitsch Rating: 2/5

Ghayal (1990)

Producer: Dharmendra (Vijayta Films). Director: Raj Kumar Santoshi.

Cast: Sunny Deol, Meenakshi Sheshadri, Amrish Puri, Raj Babbar, Moushumi Chatterjee, Kulbhushan Kharbanda, Om Puri, Shabbir Khan, Sudesh Berry, Mitwa.

Ishtory: A young educated man trying to lead a respectable life and career is trapped in a web of circumstances beyond his control. His brother gets involved with a crooked politician who has a stake in drug running and other unofficial ventures. When the brother is murdered, the hero is framed for his murder, and both the police and law courts conspire to find him guilty. Outraged and seeking revenge on the men responsible for his brother's death, the hero turns into a Rambo-like vigilante determined to root out the evil in the system. Do I even have to say it? He gets his man.

Comment: Sunny Deol's career, launched so successfully with *Betaab* had floundered after his last hit, *Arjun*. Papa Dharmendra produced *Ghayal* to resurrect beta Sunny's career, hiring promising new director Raj Kumar Santoshi for the job. Sunny's character in the film was an amalgam of his screen image and an update of Amitabh Bachchan's famous Vijay persona. Instead of turning to crime, the hero in *Ghayal* takes up arms against the system, violently attacking the corrupt men in high places whom he blames for the failure of justice and democracy. The film, although handled as a potboiler action melodrama, packs a powerful social message. The corruption depicted is genuine and omnipresent, hence the huge success of the film and its endorsement by Government and official sources. Besides firmly re-establishing Sunny Deol as an action hero for the 90s—a persona he's successfully maintained with the recent record-busting hit *Gadar—Ghayal* also made the action film respectable once more, after the tons of trashy B-movies that had exhausted audiences through the 80s.

Highlights: Sunny being chained, humiliated and tortured as he struggles, Rambo-like, against his restraints—a standard sequence in several Sunny Deol films. Raj Kumar Santoshi's script and direction.

More Like This: Arjun, Dacait, Ghatak.

Kiss-Kitsch Rating: 3/5

Roja (1993)

Producer: K Balachander (Kavithalya Productions). Director: Mani Ratnam.

Cast: Arvind Swamy, Madhoo, Pankaj Kapoor.

Ishtory: The story by Sujata and screenplay by Mani Ratnam were based on a real event: the kidnapping of an Indian Oil Corporation employee while in terrorist-ravaged Kashmir. In the film, the victim is a businessman travelling on assignment in Kashmir, accompanied by his new wife. After her husband is kidnapped, she faces a nightmarish situation: Stranded in a state where nobody speaks her language and being Hindu is reason enough to get her killed, she struggles to get her husband back.

Comment: This is the only non-Hindi film to be reviewed in this book. That's because although the film was made in Tamil, director Mani Ratnam decided to dub it in Hindi and chance a national release. His gamble paid off. His Tamil films had been garnering huge acclaim for years and were already cult hits in several pockets of the country. *Roja* was the perfect vehicle to expose his considerable talents to the mainstream Hindi film audience. The Kashmir problem was as controversial an issue to Indians as Vietnam once was to Americans. Film-makers had stayed away from the subject, believing that a controversy would harm any attempt to make a film on the issue. Mani Ratnam took exactly the opposite standpoint, a practice he's now notorious for: He made the most controversial film on Kashmir possible within the mainstream commercial cinema format. He even compromised on the character and story—in the original Tamil version, the heroine's plight is highlighted by the fact that she can't speak a word of Hindi-Urdu; by dubbing the film in Hindi, this major element was negated! But Mani Ratnam spun a story that was unpredictable. Hindi film audiences had no idea what would happen next in this unusually structured story that didn't conform to any Bollywood script conventions. *Roja* took the country by storm, starting a national controversy over scenes such as the burning of the Indian tricolour and the alleged Pakistan-bashing. Interestingly, the stars of the film, Arvind Swamy and Madhoo, tried without success to follow up their Hindi film career, while everybody else involved were in hot demand. Mani Ratnam continued his controversial, in-your-face, reality-based films with *Bombay* and *Dil Se*, but never again achieved the acclaim and success of his first crossover success.

Highlights: AR Rehman's hit songs, especially 'Roja jaaneman,' and his sweeping orchestral background score. This was the first major hit film to eschew the noisy intrusiveness of Hindi film scores for a more Western, epic feel. Santosh Sivan's cinematography. Mani Ratnam's glossy directorial style, almost as sharp as an ad film in its framing and composition.

More Like This: Mission Kashmir, Fiza.
Kiss-Kitsch Rating: 4/5

A Kiss Before Dying (With Laughter)

Two films marked a step forward. Not a revolutionary one at all, but
an important one. One was a melodramatic revenge thriller with all the
hallmarks of an Amitabh Bachchan 'Vijay' movie, with one shocking difference—the hero kills the heroine mid-film. The other was a film in
which the producer saved a ton of moolah by cutting out expensive supporting comic actors and making the heroes the buffoons, full time!
Baazigar and *Aankhen* spawned two new genres. One was the anti-hero
film in which a male lead could do anything with no limits. The other was
the out-and-out comedy film as the genre came to be called. It was no
coincidence that the lead players of both films, Shah Rukh Khan and
Govinda, went on to dominate the biz from their respective corners of the
ring, nor that the two of them never appeared in a single film together.
Bollywood had polarised at last, creating different audiences for different
kinds of films. But need we even add? They still had romance, songs,
dances and a young lead pair. The range of flavours had expanded from 1
to 31. But they were all still flavours of vanilla!

Baazigar (1993)

Producer: Ratan Jain (Venus). Director: Abbas-Mastan.

Cast: Shah Rukh Khan, Kajol, Shilpa Shetty, Dalip Tahil, Rakhee.

Ishtory: A young man is haunted by memories of his family's ruin. His
father, a rich businessman, was defrauded by an unscrupulous friend,
who took over his business and left him a pauper. As a result, the hero's
father and baby sister died of illness, too poor to even afford medicines or
a doctor, and his mother went insane. Grown now, the young man comes
to Bombay determined to avenge himself, first by destroying the villain's
family and then taking over his wealth. He accomplishes the first by
romancing and then murdering the villain's daughter. When the girl's sister suspects foul play and starts investigating, he starts to romance her as
well, insinuating himself into the father's good graces at the same time.
In the end, he kills the bad guy but sustains mortal wounds, dying in his
mother's arms while the villain's daughter looks on tearfully.

Comment: Baazigar and *Darr* were the one-two punch thrown by
stage/TV actor Shah Rukh Khan at Bollywood, blasting his way through
a series of initial flops to the most sensational success witnessed since the
meteoric rise of Amitabh Bachchan after *Zanjeer*. Bachchan had established the archetype of anti-hero successfully, and the 80s were domi-

nated by heroes who committed mayhem and murder without remorse. But they had always killed bad guys, and then too in the name of the law or vigilante justice. *Baazigar* was the first film to show a hero murdering the heroine! The moment when Shah Rukh Khan pushes Shilpa Shetty over the high-rise terrace was one of the defining moments of Hindi film. The actor playing the police inspector investigating the apparent suicide in the film, a forgettable minor role, actually went on record several times claiming he was starring as the hero of the film! Yet the glory went to Shah Rukh Khan, who turned a revenge-obsessed woman-murdering psychopath into a sympathetic, even desirable hero. By the time the other sister played by Kajol discovers that her new fiancé is the killer of her sister and is about to murder her father as well, you're rooting for him, not them! The film was Bollywood at its most kitsch.

Highlights: The songs—'Baazigar O Baazigar' with Shah Rukh Khan in a Zorro costume. The song 'Kitaabe bahut si,' a clever rip-off of the pop instrumental classic 'Popcorn.' The mirror scene with Shah Rukh Khan showing one brown and one green eye—shades of Amitabh Bachchan in *Satte Pe Satta*. Shilpa Shetty in her first major appearance (and with too much make-up)—who would have thought this ugly duckling would metamorphose (with a great make-over) into one of the hottest sex symbols in Bollywood? Johnny Lever's howlarious overblown comedy interludes. They were so popular and people kept asking to see them that he decided to appear in high-priced stage shows and make a few bucks doing them.

More Like This: Darr, Anjam, Baadshah.
Kiss-Kitsch Rating: 3/5

Aankhen (1993)

Producer: Pahlaj Nihalani (Chiragdeep International). Director: David Dhawan.

Cast: Govinda, Chunky Pandey, Shilpa Shirodkar, Ritu Shivpuri, Raageshwari, Kadar Khan, Shakti Kapoor, Raj Babbar, Macmohan.

Ishtory: A comedy of errors, this is loosely inspired by the 1973 hit comedy *Do Phool*, owes more than a little credit to Hollywood screwball comedies especially Dean Martin and Bing Crosby's *Road* series, and there's a nod to Kishore Kumar for good measure. Two young, rich buffoons, Munnu and Bunnu, get involved in a conspiracy to replace a Chief Minister with a lookalike. Meanwhile, Munnu's country cousin, who also happens to be a lookalike of Munnu, arrives in the big city and is mistaken for the real Munnu. The city Munnu happens to visit the country cousin's village at the same time where he's mistaken for the country cousin! Finally, everything is cleared up in a 'hail-hail-the-gang's-all-here' climax. But only after the two heroes confuse the hell out of the bad guys, their families, their sweethearts and most memorably, a monkey!

Comment: Hindi films have always had separate slots for heroes, heroines, comedians, vixens, sister-types, brother-types, fathers and mothers, villains and so on. After the angry-young-man trend of the 70s and 80s, it was hard enough weaving in a convincing romantic track let alone adding a comic scene or two for relief. *Aankhen* broke the trend, creating the first modern, comic hero of Bollywood: Govinda. Like his US counterparts, Jim Carrey or Robin Williams, Govinda was a versatile and gifted actor whose physical grace—he was an excellent dancer—was matched by a wild, mad streak that was better suited to comedy than the brooding action stunts of most other heroes. Director David Dhawan, a graduate of the Film and Television Institute of India (FTII), had ambitions of becoming a serious film-maker. But the success of *Aankhen* and his subsequent string of comedy hits—continuing even today with the recent success of *Biwi No. 1* and *Jodi No. 1*—typecast him as the comedy specialist of the biz. *Aankhen* is one long laughfest meant strictly for those who enjoy the 'dumb hero' brand of comedy that's become so hugely popular in the USA with films by the Farelly Brothers and a whole spate of teenage sexy/dumb hits. The two heroes camp it up in every scene, as bouncy and energetic as their monkey mascot, and you can't help but have a ball with them. While the other players in the film all sank back into obscurity, Govinda and director David Dhawan shot to superstar status, becoming an inseparable hit team for several years—including the 'No. 1' films. Apparently, Govinda over-committed himself, signing on for a staggering 50-plus films at one go according to some reports, and gained notoriety for unpunctuality and starry tantrums. After briefly reigning at the top and winning over the critics with his superbly timed comic/dramatic lead roles, he was overshadowed by Sanjay Dutt and Salman Khan, who took a cue from him and did comedy star turns far more successfully.

Highlights: The monkey.

More Like This: Chalti Ka Naam Gaadi, Do Phool, Bombay To Goa, Shola Aur Shabnam, Coolie No. 1, Hero No. 1, Judwaa, Biwi No. 1, Hera Pheri, Jodi No. 1

Kiss-Kitsch Rating: 3/5

Four Weddings
And A Bandit Queen's Funeral

A new generation and a new kind of film. No more artistic experiments. Just more of what we like and cut out all the stuff we don't like, please. So, if you were young, of a marrying age, and were fascinated by the highly romanticised ritual of Indian weddings, what could be cooler than a three-hour plus wedding video with 15 (count them, 15!) songs and dances? On the other hand, if you had grown up watching slick Western films and wondered why Hindi films couldn't be more realistic and on the edge, no problem—here's a potential Foreign Film Oscar contender. It was a crazy period in Bollywood and India. The new consumer boom had turned the country into one enormous Mall Of America, yet there was an even greater longing for all things ethnic and traditional. It took a new, young band of film-makers to deliver the new, improved brand of Bollywood product, guaranteed to cure those economic/transitional blues in just under three hours.

Hum Aapke Hain Koun (1994)

Producers: Kamal Barjatya, Raj Barjatya, Ajit Barjatya (Rajshri Productions). Director: Sooraj Barjatya.

Cast: Madhuri Dixit, Salman Khan, Mohnish Behl, Renuka Shahane, Alok Nath, Reema Lagoo, Ajit Vachchani.

Ishtory: Prem and Nisha's siblings are getting married. Being from a North Indian joint family (a large extended family living together, usually under the same roof, mansion or farmhouse), the nuptials are a long, drawn-out affair, involving several elaborate rituals and festivities. Since it's customary for the bride's siblings and groom's siblings to tease and flirt with one another, there's a lot of tomfoolery. Somewhere along the way, this mischief turns to love. But when the marriage ends, so does the romance. It's a traditional joint family and the notion of a love marriage is unthinkable. A year passes. Things take a tragic turn when the recently-married bride dies in an accident, leaving the new husband a widower with a small child to raise. As is customary in North Indian joint families, the elders decide to marry Nisha off to her widowed brother-in-law, for the sake of the infant. Unable to go against the wishes of their elders, both lovers silently prepare for the event. But in the nick of time the widowed groom-to-be learns about the romance. He sets things right and the wedding that takes place involves the right couple. Hurrah!

74

Comment: So you thought the West got wedding disease in the mid-90s, with films like *Four Weddings And A Funeral, The Wedding Singer, Muriel's Wedding, My Best Friend's Wedding* and the recent *The Wedding Planner*? Well, buddies, sorry to burst your bubble but India saw it coming first! Young director Sooraj Barjatya, inheritor of the Rajshri label—one of the last major independent film production houses in the country—and helmer of the previous hit *Maine Pyar Kiya*, somehow decided that he wanted to make a wedding film. Indian North Indian weddings are a huge affair, the brightest event in most people's lives, and attending such an event leaves everyone with a warm, fuzzy feeling for months afterward (and that's not just the hangover). So, he thought, why not capture that same good feeling in a movie, making the audience feel like they were part of the family? He was helped by the fact that a whole generation of teenage Indian boys and girls, Western-educated and sophisticated, were coming of age and learning to admire and respect their traditions and customs. He was also helped by the fact that he had a bound script, as rare in Bollywood as the Holy Grail at a Jewish convention. This was going to be one mother of a wedding video, but it was going to be scripted every step of the way. Casting his discovery Salman Khan, who had been out in the wilderness since his debut hit *Maine Pyar Kiya*, and shrewdly choosing the reigning female superstar Madhuri Dixit (she got top billing over the hero, another rarity), he set about making a film that would change Hindi film history. The story goes that he hummed bits of the background score and songs between scenes. Good songs can 'open' a film as effectively as any star, bad music can kill a hit. When completed, *Hum Aapke Hain Koun* had fifteen songs, more than twice the number usually seen in contemporary Hindi films, although two were later cut from release prints. At over three hours, the film has an entire wedding unfold before your eyes. Audiences went back for multiple viewings, wishing the experience could last forever. The songs are now a staple of real-life weddings. Salman Khan's dead-in-the-water career got a new lease of life. The Barjatya family, once known for their low-budget family dramas, became the numero uno film family, with the film allegedly becoming the top-grossing Hindi film of all time, for a while at least. And a wedding song or scene became mandatory in every second Hindi film and Hindi pop music video afterwards, with at least two other major hits spinning off successfully from the romance-and-wedding formula. So forget Adam Sandler, J Lo and Cameron Diaz. This was the one that set the wedding trend! It also set the trend for long titles shortened to acronyms: Say *HAHK* to any Hindi film fan and she'll know you're hip!

Highlights: Composer Ram/Laxman's songs (one member of the duo died, yet he persists in retaining his late partner's name), especially 'Didi tera devar diwaana,' 'Wah wah Ramji,' 'Joote de do paise le lo,' 'Dhiktana,' 'Maaya ni maaya' and 'Chocolate, lime juice.' The supporting cast—over 30 memorable characters, all of whom made an impact. The absence of a traditional villain. The highly risky yet successful casting against type of Mohnish Behl, usually a villainish sidekick, as a positive character. Sooraj Barjatya's direction, a fascinating mixture of kitsch sit-com and low-budget family drama.

More Like This: Nadiya ke Paar, Maine Pyar Kiya, Hum Saath Saath Hain, Pardes, Taal, Dilwale Dulhaniya Le Jayenge.

Kiss-Kitsch Rating: 4/5

Bandit Queen (1994)

Producer: Bobby Bedi (for Channel Four). Director: Shekhar Kapur.

Cast: Seema Biswas, Nirmal Pandey, Manoj Bajpai, Rajesh Vivek.

Ishtory: Mala Sen's screenplay was based on her biography of real-life Indian dacoit Phoolan Devi. As is painfully common in the desolate rural areas of North/Central India, upper-caste ruffians go on a rape-and-murder spree. Among their victims is a young girl who is stripped, gang-raped and forced to parade at gunpoint before the entire village. Brutalised repeatedly, she loses human perspective and grows up to bear arms and take revenge on the clan who humiliated her. The mass murder makes her a dacoit on the run from the law. Fleeing into the labyrinthine ravines of Madhya Pradesh, she and her gang fight, feud, squabble and survive until the relentless circle of violence cuts down everyone around her. Her final surrender of arms to the authorities under the terms of the general pardon granted by the Government marks the end of the film. Ironically, at the time of this book's writing, the real Bandit Queen's story came to a tragic end: After her pardon, she had become the tool of political forces, rising to the stature of a Minister of Parliament. In July 2001, she was gunned down outside her official residence in the heart of New Delhi's bureaucratic neighbourhood. A suspect apprehended soon after claimed that he had assassinated her to take revenge for her murder of his high-caste comrades. The circle had finally been closed, tragically.

Comment: The film that put Bollywood cinema on the map and was denied an Oscar due to Indian political manoeuvring. Director Shekhar

Kapur had a chequered career in Bombay's kitsch Hindi film industry, helming the hits *Masoom* and *Mr India* before going onto a series of unfinished ventures and disputes with producers over artistic control. He had turned almost full-time to producing and directing advertising films for a living when Bobby Bedi, a Delhi producer associated with the UK's Channel Four, came to him with the proposal to make *Bandit Queen*. Farokh Dhondy, then the man in charge of all things Indian at Channel Four, wanted Mala Sen's biography adapted into a television docudrama. The budget was limited but sufficient by Indian standards, and Shekhar Kapur would finally have a chance to make a film outside the rigid commercial constraints of Bollywood. Even so, *Bandit Queen* was plagued with problems from the word go. Kapur later claimed he had found it impossible to work with the British technical crew provided for him and insisted on bringing in his cameraman, Ashok Mehta, to complete the job. His first choice for the lead role, stage and art film actress Mita Vashist, turned down the controversial role, leaving him with a giant void to fill. While watching a stage performance by students of the National School of Drama (NSD) in Delhi, he spotted Seema Biswas and knew he had found his Phoolan Devi. He's said to have immersed himself into the role along with his heroine, spending days locked in a dark room imagining the horrors of gang rape (he visualised himself being repeatedly sodomised) before trying to capture the horror of Phoolan Devi's life and actions on film. The film was a raw, brutal slice of cinematic life, oozing a vitality of emotion not seen on the Hindi screen since Mahesh Bhatt's *Arth* and perhaps in a different way, Govind Nihalani's *Ardh Satya*. More harrowing than the on-screen horrors was the knowledge that every Indian viewer had, that all this was real, that it still happens today in villages around the country—the newspapers are full of it. The Indian censors took strong exception to the relentless stream of Hindi swearing but the film was only being true to life. Still, Indian audiences, disturbed by the harsh reflection of reality on screen—what a change it was from the kitsch cotton candy fantasies of most Bollywood films—jeered at the stream of Hindi abuses and whistled in encouragement during the rape scenes. Despite several harsh cuts, political manoeuvring in Government circles prevented the film from being sent as the official Indian entry for the Best Foreign Film category at the Academy Awards. Perhaps because this was not the India they wanted the world to see... In a final twist of irony, Phoolan Devi, supported by a women's group, campaigned for a ban on the film, claiming that it unacceptably distorted the facts of her life. With her death in July 2001, the film remains the closest thing to the truth of her remarkable story.

Highlights: Seema Biswas' method-actor performance—although, she was quick to clarify later that the nude scenes were done by a body double. Nirmal Pandey's powerful performance as her lover. Nusrat Fateh Ali Khan's mesmerising Indian classical music score, which impressed foreign viewers of the film and was later used in several Hollywood films like *Dead Man Walking*. Ashok Mehta's photography captured the brutality of the Central Indian landscape and the brutality of the people. Ranjit Kapoor's realistic dialogue, abusive language and all, probably the first time a Hindi film had ever captured the profane crudeness of everyday Hindi speech.

More Like This: Mother India, Mujhe Jeene Do, Dacait.

Kiss-Kitsch Rating: 4/5

Dilwale Dulhaniya Le Jayenge (1995)

Producer: Yash Chopra (Yashraj Films). Director: Aditya Chopra.

Cast: Shah Rukh Khan, Kajol, Amrish Puri, Anupam Kher, Farida Jalal, Satish Shah, Himani Shivpuri.

Ishtory: Two young London-based NRI (Non Resident Indian) brats meet up on a tour of Europe and fall in love. As with most first-generation NRIs, her father is fiercely determined to marry her to "a good Indian boy" back in their home town in Punjab. When he learns about her brush with romance, he promptly jets the family back home where he arranges his daughter's wedding with the loutish son of an old friend. Our NRI hero, pining sorely for his tour mate, follows her back to India and confesses his undying love for her. She's willing to elope, but he refuses, insisting that he will win over her family and marry her with traditional Indian pomp and ceremony. Then begins his campaign to win over the hearts of her family, a hard task since the preparations for her wedding to the other guy are already in full swing! Since at heart he is a genuine good Indian boy, he succeeds, but her father still resists. A climactic revelation changes the stern patriarch's mind at the nth moment (to use a Hindi phrase) and the lovers are united in holy matrimony!

Comment: Producer/director Yash Chopra apparently commissioned his grown son Aditya Chopra to come up with a script idea for himself to direct. But when beta Aditya narrated the germ of this story, papa Yash was unimpressed. Only then did Aditya consider directing the film himself. As things turned out, *DDLJ*, as *Dilwale Dulhaniya Le Jayenge* came to be known in the wake of the *HAHK (Hum Aapke Hain Koun)* wave of acronyms, became the biggest box-office and critical hit in Yash Chopra's career. He produced the film, which was clearly inspired by *HAHK*'s 'wedding-mania' success the year before, and lent the production a gloss that *HAHK* never had. Aditya also managed to direct two young but highly experienced stars, Shah Rukh Khan and Kajol, into delivering their best performances yet. With this film, Shah Rukh effectively changed his 'scary loverboy' image of *Baazigar* and *Darr* to launch a new 'unstoppable loverboy' phase, making him the biggest young superstar in the biz. *DDLJ* also cleverly combined both the glamour of foreign locations and lifestyles, a staple in Bollywood films, with the earthy robustness of traditional Punjabi living. *DDLJ* ran past the 250-week mark in several theatres (matinee shows only, after the first year or so) and the theme of young Westernised-educated lovers dealing with traditional family values, rather than the cliché villains with guns, became a firmly established formula in Bollywood. *DDLJ* also proved that the NRI market, mainly in the USA and UK, was commercially viable for Bollywood film-makers.

Highlights: The music score by non-starry composers Jatin/Lalit, especially 'Tujhe dekha to yeh jaana sanam,' 'Mehandi lagaake rakhna,' 'Mere khwabon mein jo aaye,' 'Ho gaya hai tujhko to pyar sajana,' 'Zaraa sa jhoom loon main' and 'Ghar aaja pardesi'—believe it or not, none of the songs or the score won any major awards, something nobody has been able to explain satisfactorily since the music was a major sellout and hugely popular and most film awards are supposedly based on audience polling. Aditya Chopra's buddy Karan Johar's uncredited directorial assist on the film—he also appears briefly as Shah Rukh Khan's chubby friend. Father Anupam Kher and son Shah Rukh Khan's unusually casual and friendly relationship, never before seen in Hindi films, especially in the hilarious scene where papa Kher congratulates son Khan on failing his graduate examinations!

More Like This: Dil To Pagal Hai, Taal, Pardes, Kuch Kuch Hota Hai.

Kiss-Kitsch Rating: 5/5

Rangeela (1995)

Producer/Director: Ramgopal Varma (Varma Corporation).

Cast: Jackie Shroff, Aamir Khan, Urmila Matondkar, Gulshan Grover.

Ishtory: A wannabe actress dreams of making it big in Hindi films someday. Encouraged by her childhood friend, a loveable broke ruffian, she struggles on hopelessly. When a top heroine is unexpectedly dropped from a film, she gets her big break. Starring opposite a major male star and sex symbol, she takes her first step to stardom. Her male co-star shows a keen interest in guiding her career, confident that she has what it takes to succeed. Suddenly, her superstar co-star seems to be in love with her, and her childhood friend admits he has always loved her. While dealing with the sudden fame and success being thrust at her, she also has to decide between the two most important men in her life.

Comment: Unusually, *Rangeela* marked the start of a famous and successful director/star pairing, rather than the hero/heroine pairing that normally followed a hit film. Director Ramgopal Varma and actress Urmila Matondkar had worked together on *Drohi*, and both had made other films separately, without much success. Allegedly a real-life couple (nobody knows for sure, even today), they collaborated on *Rangeela*, putting pieces of their experience into this delightfully unaffected romantic comedy. Even though *Rangeela* was centred almost wholly around the three main characters, each of the three was so well developed that you never felt any need for sub-plots or extraneous asides. Aamir Khan, considered a typical 'chocolate face' loverboy type until now, proved he could act like the blazes: his career has never looked back since. Urmila shot to stardom overnight, and with a style make-over by costumer Manish Malhotra, becoming a national pin-up girl. There's no question that director Varma took special care to promote her, even inviting a posse of press photographers to the beach location where a major song sequence was being shot and seeing to it that those pictures of a svelte new Urmila in that famous black swimsuit were splashed all across town. Whatever his motivation, the ploy worked brilliantly. AR Rehman, a South Indian ad jingle composer, had already made his mark as a composer in Bollywood. *Rangeela* was one of his biggest successes, contributing hugely to the film's success. Ironically, Aamir Khan and Urmila never appeared together again, mainly because she became a mainstay of Ramgopal Varma films—a collaboration that has continued successfully till today, with the recent hits *Jungle* and *Pyar Tune Kya Kiya*—and he fell out with Ramgopal Varma before *Rangeela*'s release. The fallout apparently happened when Aamir Khan, known for his high standards and expectations, commented in a pre-release interview that *Rangeela* was an average film. Director Ramgopal Varma apparently countered in another interview that Aamir Khan was an average actor, and that even the waiter (an extra in one scene) had performed better than Aamir! The resulting crossfire in the media read like a scene straight out of *Rangeela*. *Rangeela* remains an insightful, if slightly caricaturish, look at the inner workings of contemporary Bollywood.

Highlights: Pocket-sized Urmila, no more the middle-class Maharashtrian girl of her earlier films, transforms chrysalis-like into an ultra-oomphy sex symbol. AR Rehman's music: 'Tanha tanha,' 'Yaaron sun lo zara,' 'Pyar yeh jaane kaisa hain' and the theme track 'Rangeela re.' Aamir's lovable ruffian, a role he duplicated almost identically in *Ghulam*. Gulshan Grover's campy Hindi film director waiting for his big Hollywood break. Sanjay Chhel and Neeraj Vora's enjoyable script and dialogue.

More Like This: Khubsoorat, Ghulam, Pyar Tune Kya Kiya.
Kiss-Kitsch Rating: 3/5

Kuch Kuch Hota Hai (1998)

Producer: Yash Johar (Dharma Productions). Director: Karan Johar.
Cast: Shah Rukh Khan, Kajol, Rani Mukherjee, Salman Khan, Farida Jalal, Reema Lagoo, Anjali.

Ishtory: Three young friends, a man and two women, are in a love triangle at college. Two marry, the third drifts aimlessly, unable to get over her heartache. Ten years pass. The guy is left widowed with a young daughter. Said daughter longs to see her father happy again the way he was when mama was alive. She learns about his college sweetheart and looks her up. She engineers it so she goes to a summer camp where daddy's ex-flame is a camp counsellor. Then she fixes it so that daddy comes up for a visit. Smart daughter, helped by grandma, connives situations where papa and ex-flame encounter one another intimately and inevitably, love develops. There's a minor hindrance in the form of a fiancé, but no obstacle is too great and in the end true love triumphs—little Anjali gets her new mama.

Comment: While almost 90% of the 100-plus new releases kept flopping like beached fish, along came an *HAHK* (*Hum Aapke Hain Koun*), a *DDLJ* (*Dilwale Dulhaniya Le Jayenge*) or a *KKHH* (*Kuch Kuch Hota Hai*) to empty out the cash registers. Karan Johar, son of veteran producer

Yash Johar, chaddi chum (they grew up together) of Shah Rukh Khan, Kajol and Aditya Chopra (on whose *DDLJ* he assisted uncredited and appeared in a brief role) hit on yet another variant of the young-lovers-traditional-emotions NRI-market formula. Inspired by the all-American Archie Comics (like only about two dozen other Bollywood film-makers before him), Karan Johar spun a 'What if' tale: As in, 'What if Archie loved both Betty and Veronica but ended up marrying Veronica, they had a cutesy pie daughter, but Veronica died, and then the daughter set Archie up with Betty again?' Karan Johar had enough talent to make *KKHH* an original work in its own right. He went to town on the American feel, conjuring up a college straight out of his teenage Archie Comic fantasies, and setting the bulk of the film on a summer camp that was like no camp India's ever seen (in fact, both locations were actually in Mauritius). He also used hip Westernised devices like a TV host, live interviews (where the heroine sees the hero talk directly on camera to Anjali, only he means his daughter Anjali not her) and a basketball one-on-one where the heroine manages to slamdunk while dressed in a saree (you'll never see Dennis Rodman in that one, we hope). The Westernised feel went down surprisingly well with Indian audiences, mainly because of the weepy heart-tugging button-pushing romance plot. All right, so it was *Sleepless In Seattle* set in India and shot in Mauritius but somehow, don't ask me how, it worked. And another star/son/director was born.

Highlights: Hell, the whole film was one long series of highlights. Enjoy 'em all, guys.

More Like This: Hum Dil De Chuke Sanam, Taal.

Kiss-Kitsch Rating: 4/5

Sarfarosh (1999)

Producer/Director: John Mathew Matthan (Cinematt Pictures).

Cast: Naseeruddin Shah, Aamir Khan, Sonali Bhendre, Mukesh Rishi.

Ishtory: Terrorists attack a young man's father and brother for testifying against them in a court of law. The brother is killed, the father maimed. Incensed, the young man quits his studies at medical college and joins the police force—not simply to exact revenge on the terrorists, but to wipe out terrorism! He forms a crack anti-terrorist squad and their first task is to infiltrate and smash a crime ring involving drug runners, corrupt politicians and bureaucrats, and a network of anti-national traitors and Pakistani agents. The key to destroying the ring is to bring down the leader, a charismatic community leader who conducts his terrorist activities under cover of his public persona. The squad's persistence pays off as the gang is systematically destroyed and the cop and the terrorist leader head for a climactic face-off

Comment: Until *Ardh Satya*, the police procedural as a genre didn't exist. After *Ardh Satya*, any number of me-toos (rip-offs) followed, exploiting police brutality and police corruption rather than trying honestly to depict the workings of the department. Things had reached a stage where the Indian Police Service (IPS) had begun to lodge official protests and complaints against several films for their negative depiction of police officers and constables, and even to seek outright bans on some films. When John Mathew Matthan and his team of writers researched the script for *Sarfarosh*, they decided they had to do complete justice to the force and to the film. Their intensive research resulted in a film that remains the most authentic depiction of Indian police on film. Every detail is based on actual fact. Even the story, while played for its commercial pay-offs, is credible and realistic. John Mathew Matthan, an ad film-maker at the time, decided he wanted to shoot the film in one go, unlike the Bollywood practice of shooting as and when stars were available. This meant waiting almost three years just to start shooting! It was well worth the wait. Audiences, exhausted by the overblown shenanigans of filmi cops, sensed the difference immediately. The fact that *Sarfarosh* was also a slickly-made, tensely-paced action thriller didn't hurt either. The film swept the awards, establishing John Mathew Matthan as a name director, and confirmed Aamir Khan's status as the best actor/star in the biz.

Highlights: Veteran stage and film actor Naseeruddin Shah's tour-de-force performance as the ghazal-singing terrorist head honcho. The scene in which Naseeruddin Shah bites the neck of the goat. The title sequence and final scene, especially that flippant exit line, "Warm up dinner, I'll be back," delivered by Aamir Khan before leaving to deal with the last surviving member of the gang. Jethu Mandal's editing.

More Like This: Ardh Satya, Baazi.

Kiss-Kitsch Rating: 4/5

Cricket In A Dhoti
& Other Millennial Wonders

It looks like Bollywood film-makers and audiences have started the millennium wondering why the hell they should give a damn about social realism or real-life subjects and issues. All of a sudden it has become fashionable to make good, meaningful cinema that also delivers a wallop of entertainment. Films like *Lagaan, Gadar, Ek Rishta, Aks, Yaadein*— and the forthcoming *Kabhi Khushi Kabhi Gam, Devdas* and *Ashoka The Great*, among others—have been building and toppling expectations like a house of cards. It has become impossible to predict what kind of film is going to be made next, or how successful or not it's going to be at the box office. The only thing we can tell for sure is that it's a very exciting and progressive time. Bollywood is finally finding a profitable international audience, and Hindi films are becoming better looking, better produced, better everything. We've even got used to those songs and dances!

Mohabbatein (2000)

Producer: Yash Chopra (Yashraj Films). Director: Aditya Chopra.

Cast: Amitabh Bachchan, Shah Rukh Khan, Aishwarya Rai, Uday Chopra, Preity Jhangiani.

Ishtory: A new music teacher arrives at a very plush all-boys college. His young male protégés soon discover that he has an old antagonistic relationship with the college dean. It turns out that the young music teacher used to be a student at the college, and fell in love with the dean's daughter. The father opposed the match and rusticated (expelled) him from the college without even confronting the erring student. The daughter killed herself in despair (wouldn't you, if you had a pa like that?), driving the father deeper into his iron-handed disciplinary ways. When the music teacher finds that his three favourite students are in love with three girls from a neighbouring girls college, he encourages their romance against opposition from the dean. Only after the romances turn into full-blown marriage plans does the furious dean realise that the errant music teacher is the same ex-student who fell in love with his daughter. If you think there isn't much to this story—hell, the heroine's dead before the story starts—and can't figure out why it takes three and a half hours to unfold this flimsy plotline, you're probably over 13. 13, by the way, is the average age of Hindi film-goers, as defined by Bollywood mogul Subhash Ghai.

Comment: Mohabbatein is less notable for its intrinsic merits than for its whopping success at a time of relative drought in the biz. It also marked the triumphant return of Amitabh Bachchan to the big screen in the wake of his phenomenal success as the host of *Kaun Banega Crorepati*, the Indian TV version of the British show *Who Wants To Be A Millionaire*. In India, the poorer audiences sit downstairs in the stalls while more elite viewers pay extra to sit up in the balcony and dress circle. It's traditional for audiences sitting at the front of the hall (the cheapest seats) to whistle loudly, cheer and fling coins at the screen during their favourite moments. *Mohabbatein* had the distinction of being one of the first films to see coins flung from both the balcony and stalls! And audiences quoting key lines—"Lock kiya jaye?" "Confident, sure?" "Sahi jawab!"—from Amitabh Bachchan's TV show rather than the film being screened! It was also the first pairing of the two biggest stars in Bollywood, one from the 70s/80s and the other the reigning box-office badshah (emperor)—a kind of Al Pacino/Tom Cruise face-off—and the scenes featuring both are electrifying. But the film as a whole, following three parallel love stories besides the central conflict, was one long music video, a bubblegummer's delight. NRI audiences lapped it up and so did teenage urban audiences in India. Coming after the solid entertainment mix of his earlier *Dilwale Dulhaniya Le Jayenge*, the film was a disappointing second showing by young director Aditya Chopra. In many ways it echoed the slick song-and-dance sequences of Yash Chopra's *Dil To Pagal Hai*, which Aditya Chopra co-wrote and assisted dad with, but ultimately *Mohabbatein* lacked the satisfying romantic fulfilment of that far tighter and slicker film. It also fell far short of breaking any box-office records.

Highlights: The use of several tons of gold/brown autumn leaves trucked in for several key shots. The Shah Rukh/Amitabh scenes.

More Like This: Dil To Pagal Hai.

Kiss-Kitsch Rating: 2/5

Kaho Na Pyar Hai (2000)

Producer/Director: Rakesh Roshan (Filmcraft).

Cast: Hrithik Roshan, Amisha Patel, Anupam Kher, Farida Jalal, Dalip Tahil.

Ishtory: An aspiring singer falls in love with a rich man's daughter. Daddy, in the decades-long tradition of heroine's fathers in Bollywood, rejects the suitor outright. When our sensitive young crooner persists, daddy's goons kill him. End of story. Or so you think. In an incredible plot twist, the heroine, trying hard to get over her failed romance, travels abroad and meets a man who's an identical lookalike of her dead lover! Naturally, she falls for him too—must be genetic programming. Again, Daddy steps in. But this time, our young lover's a fighter and he thrashes the hell out of those goons, avenging his lookalike's death and winning the girl.

Comment: Rakesh Roshan, a failed but well-known film actor, had a string of hit melodramas under his belt—*Khudgarz, Khoon Bhari Maang, Kishen Kanhaiya, Karan Arjun*—when he launched *Kaho Na Pyar Hai.* Unlike a long list of other illustrious star/son launch vehicles, the film was never intended to be the debut of his son, Hrithik Roshan. In fact, his first choice was Shah Rukh Khan but, as with any Bollywood star at his peak, Shah Rukh Khan was committed to several projects simultaneously and didn't have free time for another year or two. Besides, Rakesh Roshan preferred to shoot his film in one long schedule, thereby curtailing exorbitant interest costs on the finance and avoiding the ridiculous discontinuities that routinely resulted from piecemeal shooting. When meeting with his scriptwriter Honey Irani and music composer brother Rajesh Roshan to discuss fresh casting ideas, son Hrithik walked into the room, freshly gleaming from his workout. Honey Irani looked at Rakesh Roshan and said, "Why not him?" and he said, "Yes, why not!" Hrithik Roshan, a shy sensitive, highly intelligent young man, was disturbed by his father's unexpected decision, and went to his room. Rakesh Roshan followed him up and talked it over with him. Finally, Hrithik, who had plans to go abroad to the US to study 3D animation design, agreed. And a star was born! The problem didn't end there: When heroine Kareena Kapoor (sister of Karishma, granddaughter of Raj Kapoor) learned that she was to star against the producer/director's novice son instead of a major star, she walked out of the film. With shooting about to begin, Rakesh Roshan cast about desperately and hit on a Bombay student, Amisha Patel. His next hurdle was with the film's music. Brother Rajesh Roshan had delivered some excellent scores in the past, but wasn't considered a hit music director. With the music rights to a film bringing in as much earning as the box-office receipts of one major territory (like Western India, for instance), he was under great pressure to take a bigger, more saleable name. Especially since his hero and heroine were now complete unknowns. Yet he stuck by brother Rajesh, drawing out the finest score of his career. The film, released with almost no expectations or buzz—a stark contrast to the incredibly hyped launches of the last year or two—took the country by storm. Hrithik Roshan, perhaps the first Bollywood male star to have it all—looks, physique, acting talent, voice, intelligence, charm, grace, vulnerability, you name it—became the biggest superstar in the shortest time possible. A powerful, intrusive mass media—TV, Internet, FM Radio, a growing film and mainstream press—spread the news that a 'perfect 10' new male hero had arrived. *KNPH*, as *Kaho Na Pyar Hai* was instantly known, became a gigantic sensation, rapidly jostling older contenders to become the highest-grossing Bollywood film. Hrithik-mania swept the country. So massive was the film's success that weeks after the film's release underworld tough guys tried to extort huge sums from Rakesh Roshan and, when he failed to pay up, tried to assassinate him in broad daylight on a crowded public street. Rakesh Roshan was hit twice by bullets but miraculously survived. As Hrithik Roshan later confessed to an edge-of-the-seat audience at a film awards function, "I never got to celebrate my film's success because I was given pain and pleasure on the same plate." Today, a year and four releases after his debut, Hrithik remains the most awesomely talented male actor in the biz, barring only the ageing yet charismatic Amitabh Bachchan. Comparisons to fellow superstar Shah Rukh Khan are odious but you have to admit that even Shah Rukh Khan was never this good in his first film—or his first half-dozen films!—and if you do a complete checklist, Hrithik wins the star quotient prize hands down.

Highlights: Hrithik's dual-layered performance as the sensitive artistic singer and the tough manly lover. Rajesh Roshan's excellent music score: 'Ek pal ka jeena,' 'Kaho na pyar hai,' 'Pyar ke kashtee mein' and the hauntingly melodious 'Na tum jano na hum.' Singer Lucky Ali's renditions of 'Ek pal ka jeena' and 'Na tum jaano na hum'—an inspired choice by Rajesh Roshan. Producer/director Rakesh Roshan's ability to tell an exciting story through slickly shot and edited visuals, never once allowing his star son to steal the limelight (although he did so anyway), and always making the story king.

More Like This: Khoon Bhari Maang (which uses the exact same device but with the 'dead' heroine returning to take vengeance), *Karan Arjun, Baazigar, Yaadein*.

Kiss-Kitsch Rating: 4/5

Gadar: A Love Story (2001)

Producer: Nitin Keni (Zee Network). Director: Anil Sharma.

Cast: Sunny Deol, Amisha Singh, Amrish Puri, Lilette Dubey, Vivek Shauq.

Ishtory: During 1947, the year of India's Partition from Pakistan, Tara, a Sikh truck driver in Punjab (on the border of both countries) happens to meet a rich Muslim girl, Sakina. When Hindu/Muslim riots erupt, he saves her from a rampaging mob and shelters her. They fall in love, get married and even have a child. But one day she sees a picture of her father, whom she believed was killed in the riots, in a newspaper. He's now the Mayor of Lahore, a major Pakistani city, and when she contacts him, he calls her over to Pakistan. Tara and his mother want to accompany her but are not given visas. When Sakina arrives in Lahore, her father tries to make her forget India, her husband and her son, and forces her into a marriage with a Muslim boy of his choice. Tara arrives in Lahore in the nick of time—the day of her marriage—and confronts her father. He humiliates Tara and insults India unforgivably. Tara goes on a rampage, determined to get his wife back against all odds. In the end, both lovers return to India and try to build their lives anew. (Was that obvious?)

Comment: At the time of this writing, word from the trade is that *Gadar* has already broken all records in its two-month run and is poised to become the highest-grossing Hindi film of all time. It's a totally unexpected achievement, because the film had no buzz at all on release, the music was a complete flop, the producer was a television channel venturing into feature-film production for the first time, the director hadn't delivered a hit for longer than anyone could recall, the subject was a period film—a genre which rarely does well in India. If that wasn't enough, the star Sunny Deol had delivered a string of flops over the last few years. To make matters worse, the film was released on the same day as the most-talked about and awaited new release of the year, *Lagaan*. Yet *Gadar* brought Sunny Deol's North Indian fans out in droves, turning the film into his most successful ever. While in a country like America, it's common to see a hundred films made about a national crisis like, say, Vietnam, in India it's rare to see even a single major film or book about such a crisis. It's partly the national tendency to forget and move on, rather than a lack of emotional response. However, over the last decade or so, sentiment has been building powerfully about past events. The current wave of Hindu fundamentalism and Muslim-bashing, aggravated by events in the Middle East, Islamic terrorism, the Kashmir wars, has led to an explosion of interest in the past, especially Partition, the most traumatic event in the last century of India's history. It's no coincidence that both the year's biggest hits, *Gadar* and *Lagaan*, chose to deal with different aspects of the issue—*Lagaan* focussing on the rural struggle against the oppressive British rule, and *Gadar* dealing with the Hindu/Muslim issue. There have been other films and shows made on the problems of Partition before—most memorably, Govind Nihalani's made-for-television miniseries *Tamas*—but *Gadar* deals with the crisis head-on. It does not flinch from showing the brutal massacre of millions of innocents who became the scapegoats of communal madness during the evacuation of Hindus from Pakistan and Muslims from India. *Gadar* was the eye of a storm of controversy for a brief while after release, with Muslim groups demanding the film be banned for its open criticism of Muslims, and even nervous Sikh groups saying that they would prefer a ban than a backlash. But the murmurs of protest soon died down, awed by the staggering success of the film. Young educated Indians, growing up angry at the mistakes of previous Governments and generations, loved *Gadar*, adored the Muslim/Pakistan bashing and lustily cheered Sunny Deol on as he turned into a one-man Indian army.

Highlights: The effective action and stunt choreography. Sunny Deol's balanced performance—restrained when required, robust and raging when angered—is the best of his career.

More Like This: Yehudi Ki Ladki, Garam Hawa, Tamas, Pukar.

Kiss-Kitsch Rating: 4/5

Lagaan (2001)

Producer: Aamir Khan (Aamir Khan Productions). Director: Ashutosh Gowarikar.

Cast: Aamir Khan, Gracie Singh, Rachel Shelley, Paul Blackthorne, Kulbhushan Kharbhanda.

Ishtory: An update of the 50s hit *Mera Gaon Mera Desh* with significant variations. During the mid-1800s, a small village in Western India is burdened by the punishing lagaan (land levy) imposed by the ruling British. Faced by a drought, the villagers realise they can't continue to pay the lagaan and survive. They petition the local rajah, hoping to be excused from the lagaan for the year. The local British administrator, the rajah's puppet-master, ridicules the villagers' petition and suggests that if they play a cricket match against his ace team and win, he will lift the lagaan for a year, no, make that two, oh, all right, three years. Bhuvan, the young progressive spokesperson for the villagers, snatches the opportunity and agrees. The British administrator, amused, warns them that if they lose the match, the lagaan will be doubled. The villagers return, shocked at the agreement—they've never seen a cricket match, let alone played the game! The administrator's sister, overhearing the whole conversation, knows that her brother and his ace English team will decimate the villagers. She secretly sneaks down to their village and shows them the basics of the game. After that, Bhuvan and his folk work day and night—the drought makes farming impossible anyway—to master the sport. The final face-off between the British and the Indian villagers takes up over an hour of this four-hour film, and what a match it is! The result isn't obvious until the very last ball, and if you want to know who wins, you had better see it yourself. This is one story I refuse to spoil!

Comment: Director Ashutosh Gowarikar had two disastrous B-grade films under his belt, and an outrageous script idea when he approached film star Aamir Khan. The star refused to act in the film, believing that the idea was unworkable in the context of commercial Bollywood cinema. But Gowarikar believed completely in his story and set about completing the entire screenplay. When he went back to Aamir with the full script, the star was floored. Still, no major producer would have agreed to back a big-budget film about villagers in dhotis (loin clothes) playing cricket! That's when Ashutosh Gowarikar convinced Aamir Khan to produce the film himself. The star, known for his excessive involvement with the whole film-making process and his stubborn refusal to do more than two films a year—as against, say, Govinda, who at the height of his stardom had a record 50 films in the making at the same time—decided what the hell, and took the plunge. It was the smartest decision of his life and career. By backing the film himself, he was able to put his obsessive fascination with detail to good use. Every rupee spent on *Lagaan* is visible on screen and director Gowarikar's obvious love for his subject and sense of pacing turn this unlikely plot into a gripping drama, with the now famous cricket match at the climax proving to be far more thrilling than any real-life cricket match in the last ten years! *Lagaan* was a phenomenal success commercially and critically. Released on the same day as *Gadar*, it proved that Bollywood audiences will and do accept offbeat subjects if handled with the same epic flair as any formula love story or musical comedy.

Highlights: The casting—every single character is perfectly cast, with relatively unknown faces used, including the first-time heroine Gracie Singh. Aamir Khan's superb production and performance. Director Ashutosh Gowarikar's well-structured script and direction, especially his ability to turn even the smallest twitch into a nail-biting suspense moment. The reinvention of cricket by the villagers, including the 'discovery' of spin bowling and the anachronistic use of bodyline attack, is obviously fictional yet enjoyably used.

More Like This: Naya Daur, Mera Gaon Mera Desh, Jo Jeeta Wahi Siqandar, Sau Crore.

Kiss-Kitsch Rating: 5/5

Still Got Them Bollywood Blues

Still haven't had enough? There's no point listing more movies, there are just too darn many of them (thankfully!). But if you want some more sweet and lowdown on the movies, the biz, the stars, the makers, or just plain gossip and gab, here's a few books, magazines and websites you can search through. Surprisingly, there aren't many books on Bollywood, let alone many worth reading, and there are as many websites as there are fans on the net, but you can check out these suggestions in the meanwhile.

Books

Bollywood Cinema: Temples Of Desire, Vijay Mishra (Routledge, November 2001)

The Encyclopaedia Of Indian Cinema, Ashish Rajadhyaksha & Paul Willemen (Oxford University Press, 1999)

Sholay: The Making Of A Legend, Anupama Chopra (Penguin India, 2000)

Dadamoni: A Biography Of Ashok Kumar, Kishore Valicha (Penguin India, 1998)

Kishore Kumar, Kishore Valicha (Penguin India, 2000)

Magazines (English)

Stardust (editor: Ashwin Varde, monthly, Magna Publishing Co, Magna House, Old Prabhadevi Road, Prabhadevi, Bombay 400 025, India)

Filmfare (editor: Khalid Mohamed, monthly, Times of India, Times of India Bldg., DN Road, Bombay 400 001, India)

Showtime (editor: Kanan Divecha, monthly, Magna Publishing Co, Magna House, Old Prabhadevi Road, Prabhadevi, Bombay 400 025, India)

Cine Blitz (editor: Rita Mehta, monthly, Blitz Publications, 17 Patel House, Cawasji Patel Street, Fort, Bombay 400 001, India)

Trade Guide (editor: Taran Adarsh, weekly, Manek Chambers, 3rd Floor, Naaz Cinema Complex, Lamington Road, Bombay 400 004, India)

Film Information (editor: Komal Nahata, weekly, Goverdhan Bldg No. 2, 1st Floor, 478 Parekh Street, Bombay 400 004, India)

Websites

Rediff.com (www.rediff.com) has a well-written and presented, reliably informed Bollywood section

Indiatimes.com (www.indiatimes.com) has most of the official launch tie-ins.

Filmfare (www.filmfareindia.com) is the official website of the print magazine.

Stardust/Showtime (www.stardustmag.com) is the official website of the country's largest-selling print magazine.

About The Author: Ashok Banker is a well-known novelist, columnist and scriptwriter. Over 1800 of his columns and articles have appeared in virtually every major print and web publication in India. He lives in Bombay.

The Essential Library

Build up your library with new titles every month

Alfred Hitchcock by Paul Duncan

More than 20 years after his death, Alfred Hitchcock is still a household name, most people in the Western world have seen at least one of his films, and he popularised the action movie format we see every week on the cinema screen. He was both a great artist and dynamite at the box office. This book examines the genius and enduring popularity of one of the most influential figures in the history of the cinema!

Stanley Kubrick by Paul Duncan

Kubrick's work, like all masterpieces, has a timeless quality. His vision is so complete, the detail so meticulous, that you believe you are in a three-dimensional space displayed on a two-dimensional screen. He was commercially successful because he embraced traditional genres like War (*Paths Of Glory, Full Metal Jacket*), Crime (*The Killing*), Science Fiction (*2001*), Horror (*The Shining*) and Love (*Barry Lyndon*). At the same time, he stretched the boundaries of film with controversial themes: underage sex (*Lolita*); ultra violence (*A Clockwork Orange*); and erotica (*Eyes Wide Shut*).

Orson Welles by Martin Fitzgerald

The popular myth is that after the artistic success of *Citizen Kane* it all went downhill from there for Orson Welles, that he was some kind of fallen genius. Yet, despite overwhelming odds, he went on to make great Films Noirs like *The Lady From Shanghai* and *Touch Of Evil*. He translated Shakespeare's work into films with heart and soul (*Othello, Chimes At Midnight, Macbeth*), and he refused to take the bite out of modern literature, giving voice to bitterness, regret and desperation in *The Magnificent Ambersons* and *The Trial*. Far from being down and out, Welles became one of the first cutting-edge independent filmmakers.

Film Noir by Paul Duncan

The laconic private eye, the corrupt cop, the heist that goes wrong, the femme fatale with the rich husband and the dim lover - these are the trademark characters of Film Noir. This book charts the progression of the Noir style as a vehicle for film-makers who wanted to record the darkness at the heart of American society as it emerged from World War to the Cold War. As well as an introduction explaining the origins of Film Noir, seven films are examined in detail and an exhaustive list of over 500 Films Noirs are listed.

The Essential Library

Currently Available

Film Directors:

Woody Allen (£3.99)
Jane Campion (£2.99)
Jackie Chan (£2.99)
David Cronenberg (£3.99)
Alfred Hitchcock (£3.99)
Stanley Kubrick (£2.99)
David Lynch (£3.99)
Sam Peckinpah (£2.99)
Orson Welles (£2.99)
Steven Spielberg (£3.99)

Tim Burton (£3.99)
John Carpenter (£3.99)
Joel & Ethan Coen (£3.99)
Terry Gilliam (£2.99)
Krzysztof Kieslowski (£2.99)
Sergio Leone (£3.99)
Brian De Palma (£2.99)
Ridley Scott (£3.99)
Billy Wilder (£3.99)

Film Genres:

Film Noir (£3.99)
Horror Films (£3.99)
Spaghetti Westerns (£3.99)
Blaxploitation Films (£3.99)

Hong Kong Heroic Bloodshed (£2.99)
Slasher Movies(£3.99)
Vampire Films (£2.99)

Film Subjects:

Laurel & Hardy (£3.99)
Steve McQueen (£2.99)
The Oscars® (£3.99)
Bruce Lee (£3.99)

Marx Brothers (£3.99)
Marilyn Monroe (£3.99)
Filming On A Microbudget (£3.99)
Film Music (£3.99)

TV:

Doctor Who (£3.99)

Literature:

Cyberpunk (£3.99)
Hitchhiker's Guide (£3.99)
Terry Pratchett (£3.99)

Philip K Dick (£3.99)
Noir Fiction (£2.99)
Sherlock Holmes (£3.99)

Ideas:

Conspiracy Theories (£3.99)
Feminism (£3.99)

Nietzsche (£3.99)

History:

Alchemy & Alchemists (£3.99)
American Civl War (£3.99)

The Crusades (£3.99)
American Indian Wars (£3.99)

Available at all good bookstores, or send a cheque to: **Pocket Essentials (Dept BY), 18 Coleswood Rd, Harpenden, Herts, AL5 1EQ, UK**. Please make cheques payable to 'Oldcastle Books.' Add 50p postage & packing for each book in the UK and £1 elsewhere.

US customers can send $6.95 plus $1.95 postage & packing for each book to: **Trafalgar Square Publishing, PO Box 257, Howe Hill Road, North Pomfret, Vermont 05053, USA**. e-mail: tsquare@sover.net

Customers worldwide can order online at **www.pocketessentials.com**.

The Essential Library

Build up your library with new titles every month

Mike Hodges by Mark Adams, £3.99

Features an extensive interview with Mike Hodges. His first film, Get Carter, has achieved cult status (recently voted the best British film ever in Hotdog magazine) and continues to be the benchmark by which every British crime film is measured. His latest film, Croupier, was such a hit in the US that is was re-issued in the UK. His work includes crime drama (Pulp), science-fiction (Flash Gordon and The Terminal Man), comedy (Morons From Outer Space) and watchable oddities such as A Prayer For The Dying and Black Rainbow. Mike Hodges is one of the great maverick British film-makers.

Agatha Christie by Mark Campbell, £3.99

Foreword by Simon Brett. Since her debut in 1920 with The Mysterious Affair At Styles, Agatha Christie has become the chief proponent of the English village murder mystery. She created two enormously popular characters - the Belgian detective Hercule Poirot, and the inquisitive elderly spinster and amateur sleuth Miss Jane Marple of St Mary Mead – and wrote in many different genres.

As well as an informed introduction to the Christie phenomenon, this book examines all her novels and short stories. The film, TV and stage adaptations are listed, and the appendices point you to books and websites where you can find out more.

French New Wave by Chris Wiegand, £3.99

The directors of the French New Wave were the original film geeks - a collection of celluloid-crazed cinéphiles with a background in film criticism and a love for American auteurs. Having spent countless hours slumped in Parisian cinémathèques, they armed themselves with handheld cameras, rejected conventions, and successfully moved movies out of the studios and on to the streets at the end of the 1950s.

Borrowing liberally from the varied traditions of film noir, musicals and science fiction, they released a string of innovative and influential pictures, including the classics Le Beau Serge, Jules Et Jim and A Bout De Souffle. By the mid-1960s, the likes of Jean-Luc Godard, François Truffaut, Claude Chabrol, Louis Malle, Eric Rohmer and Alain Resnais had changed the rules of film-making forever.

The Hitchhiker's Guide by MJ Simpson, £3.99

Updated Edition. Foreword by Simon Jones. Based on 20 years of research and extensive interviews with the cast and crew of Hitchhiker's Guide, including the late Douglas Adams, this book also includes details of Douglas Adams' other projects (Dirk Gently, The Meaning Of Liff and Starship Titanic) plus his early work on series such as Doctor Who and Monty Python's Flying Circus.

Available at all good bookstores, or send a cheque to: **Pocket Essentials (Dept BY), 18 Coleswood Rd, Harpenden, Herts, AL5 1EQ, UK**. Please make cheques payable to 'Oldcastle Books.' Add 50p postage & packing for each book in the UK and £1 elsewhere.

US customers can send $6.95 plus $1.95 postage & packing for each book to: **Trafalgar Square Publishing, PO Box 257, Howe Hill Road, North Pomfret, Vermont 05053, USA**. e-mail: tsquare@sover.net

Customers worldwide can order online at **www.pocketessentials.com**.